FORMULA COLORING BOOK

+

F1 HISTORY, FACTS AND BEST DRIVERS RANKING

GW01425282

COLOR TEST PAGE

F1 HISTORY, DRIVERS STATS
AND FREE BONUS IS AT THE
END OF THIS BOOK, ENJOY!

F1 cars accelerate from 0 to
100 mph and go back to 0
within 4 seconds

Basic cost of a F1 car
is over $7 million

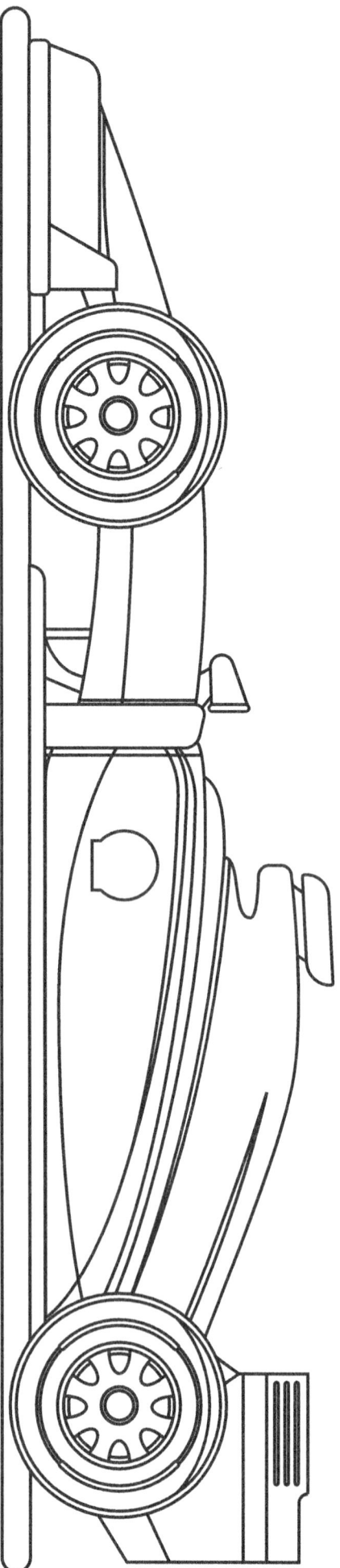

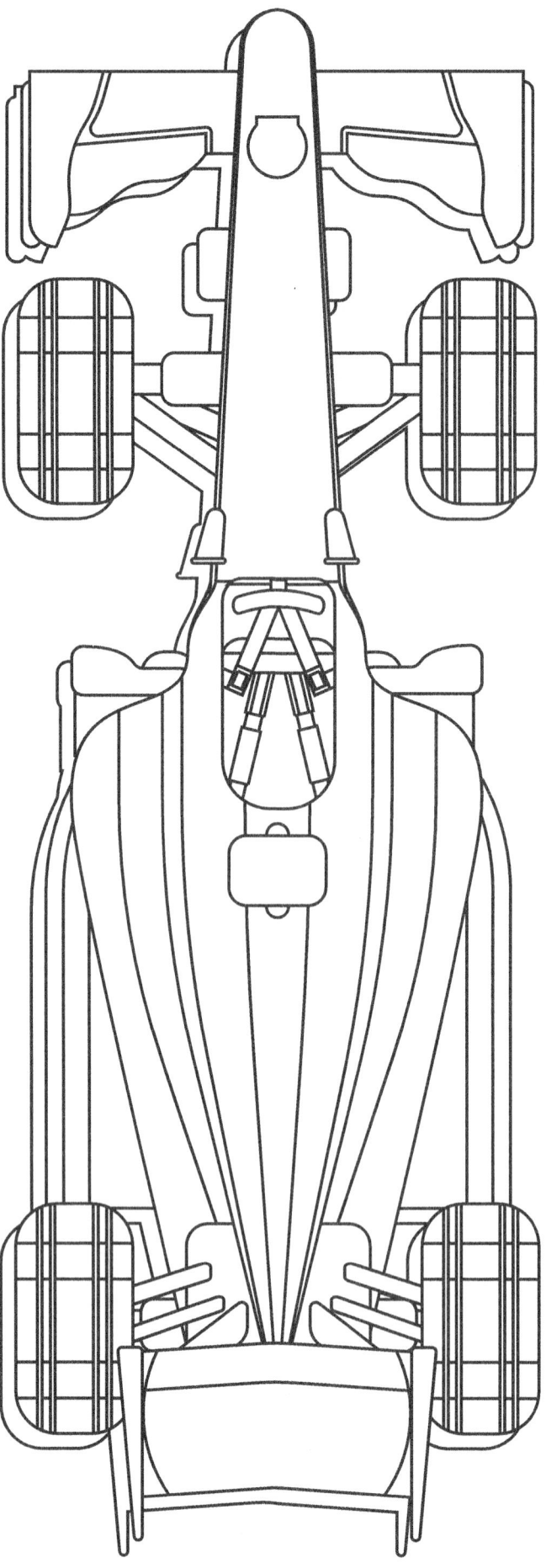

Brake discs can reach
1,000 degrees centigrade

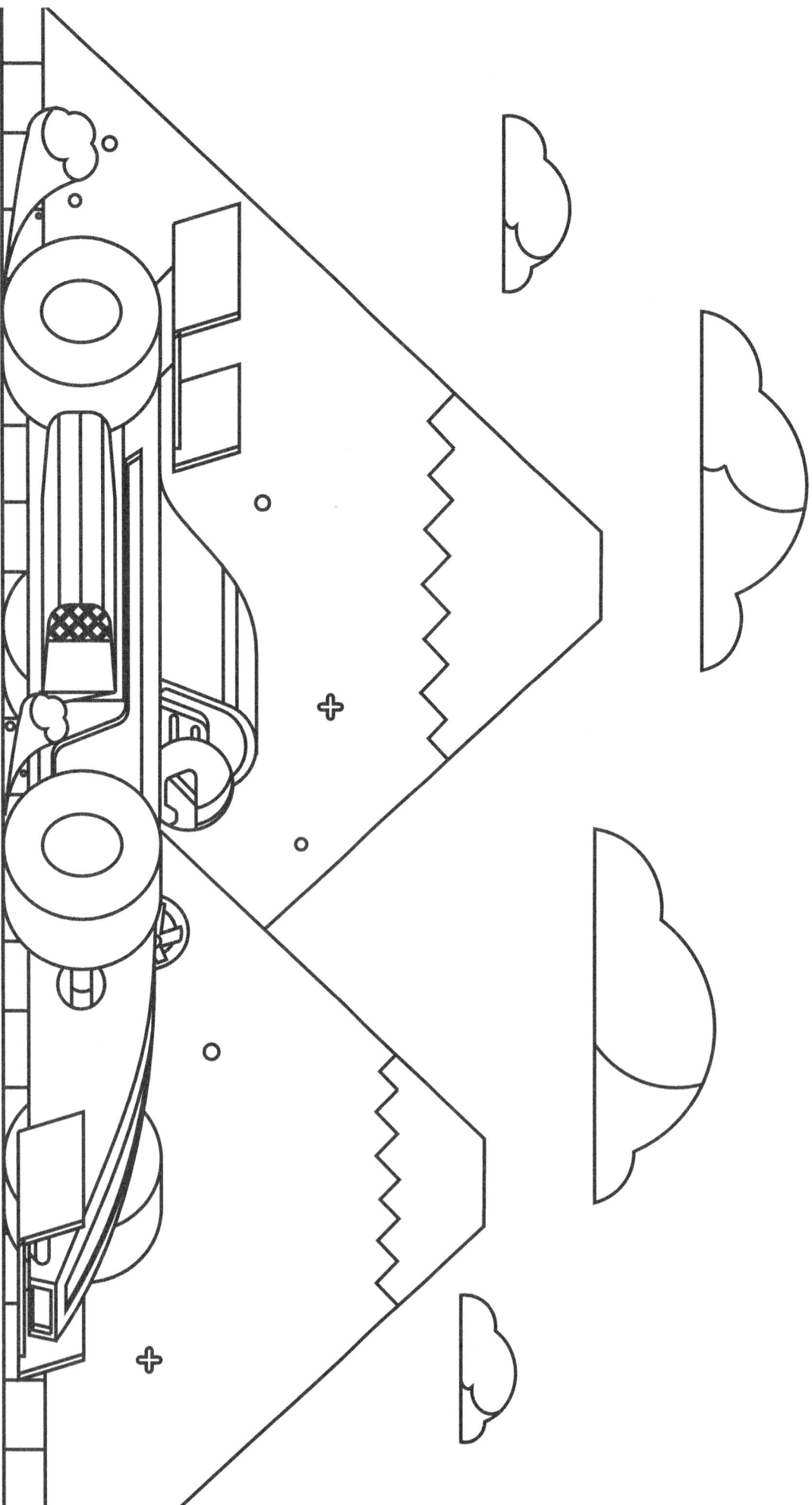

Engine can't be turned when it's cold

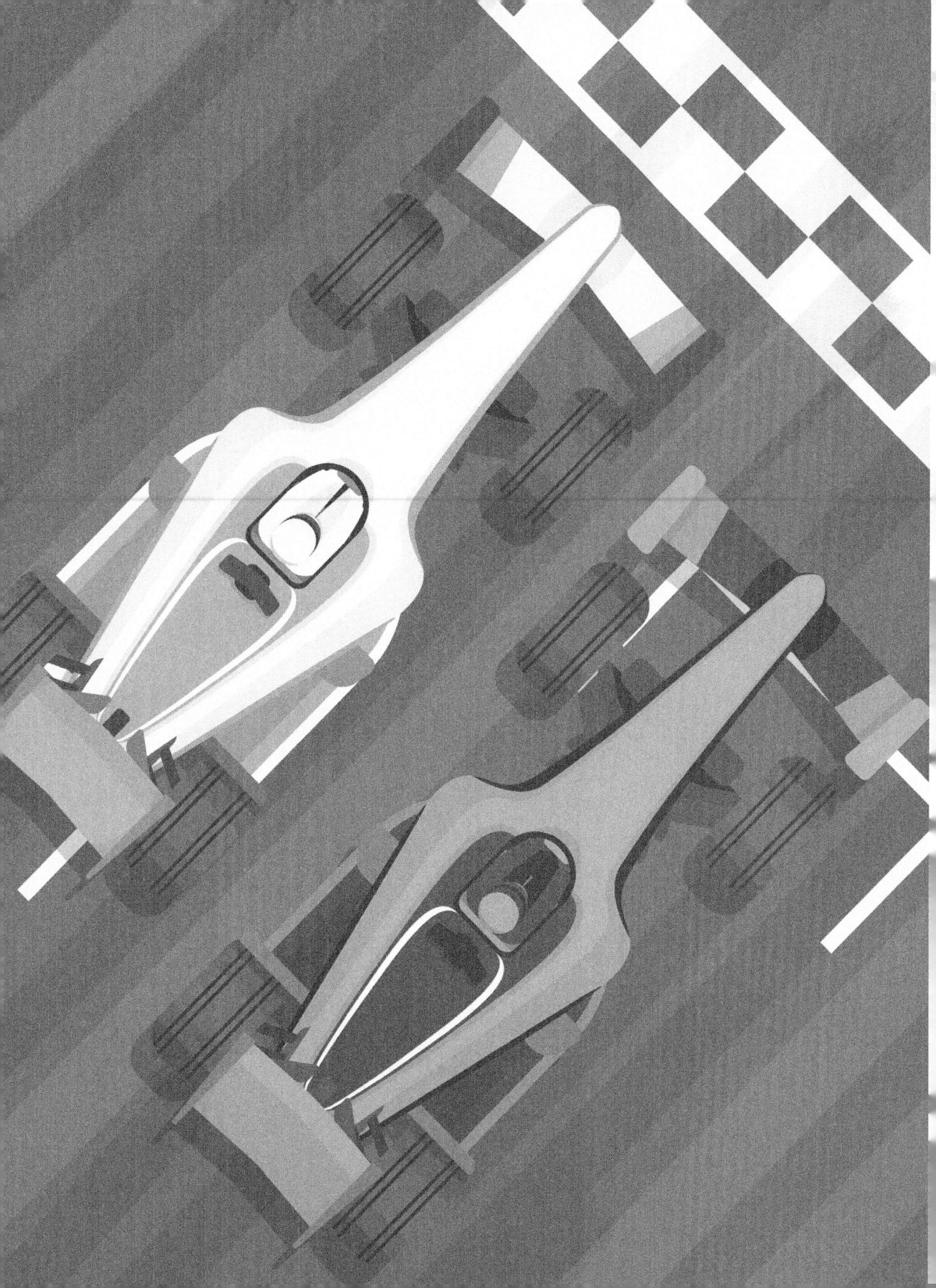

Revs up to 15,000 RPM

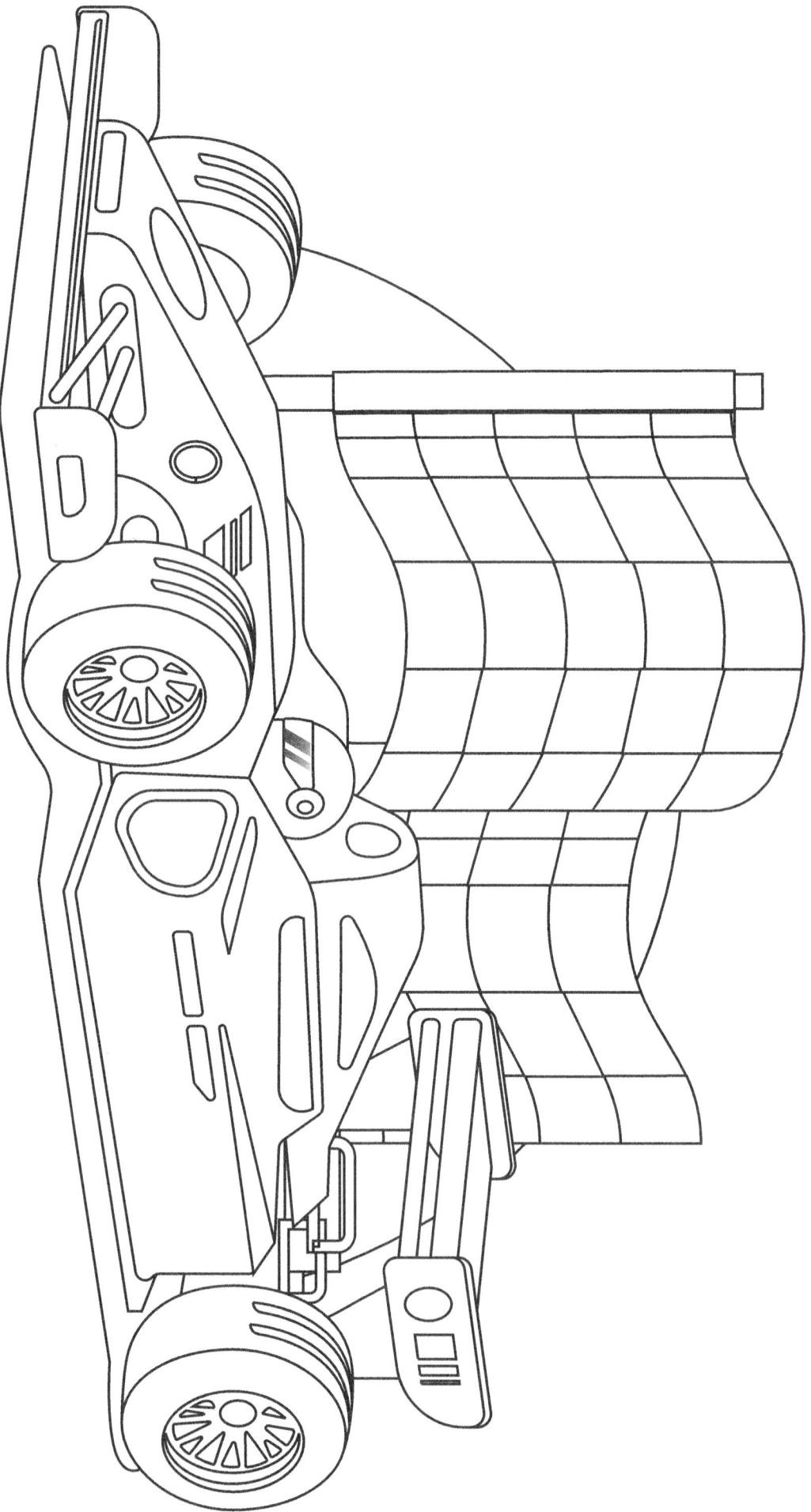

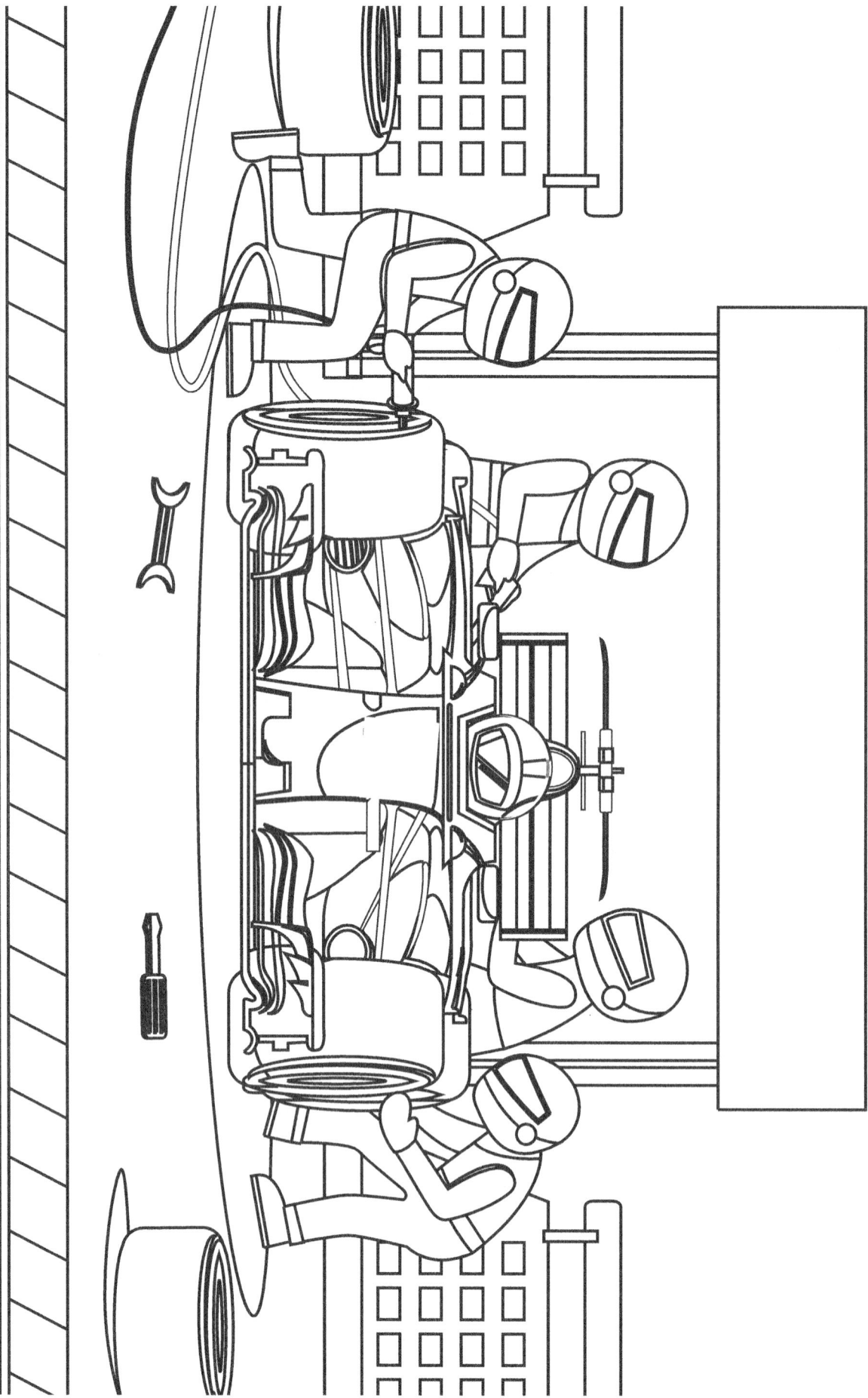

Each vehicle has 80K assembled components

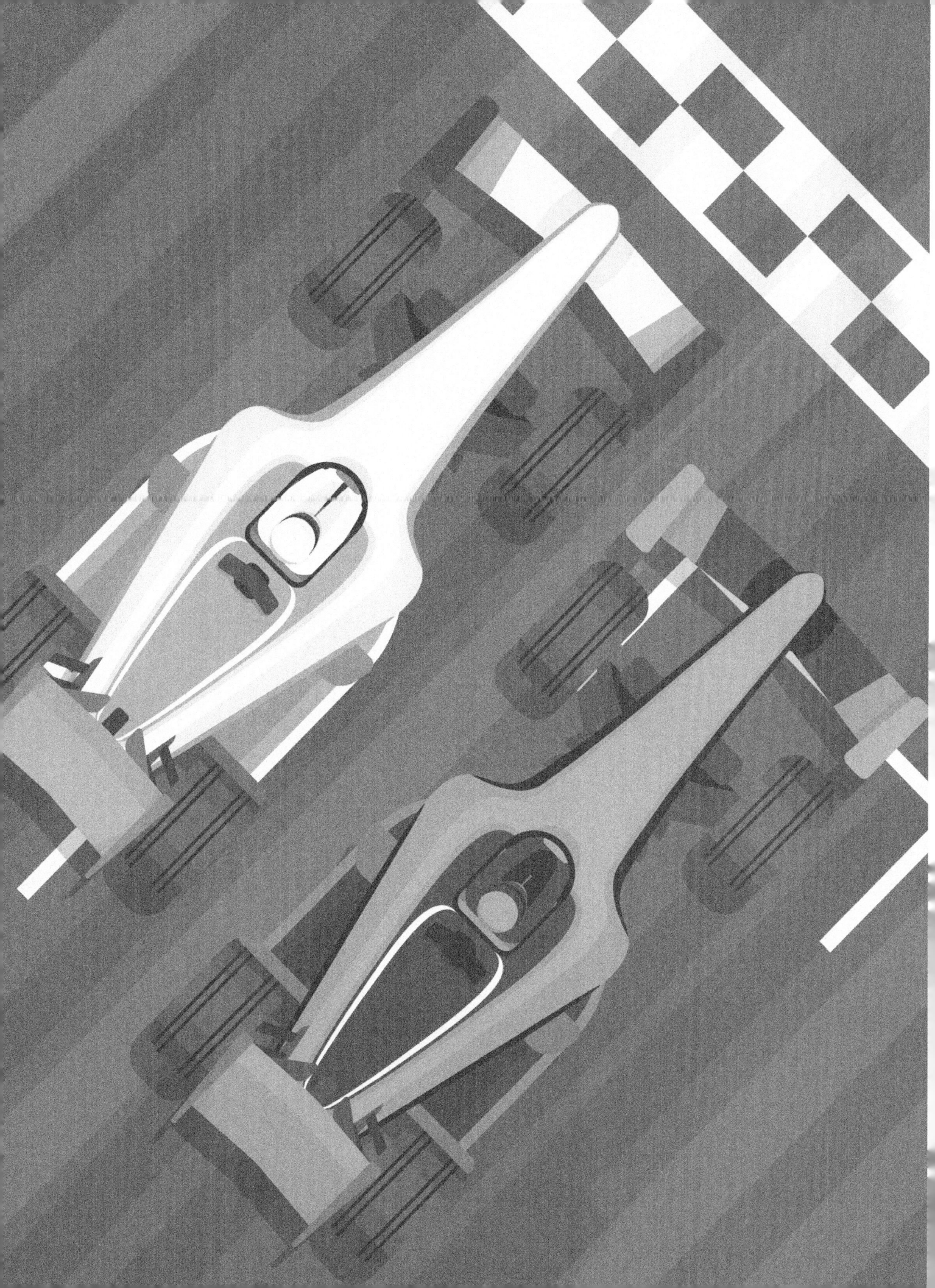

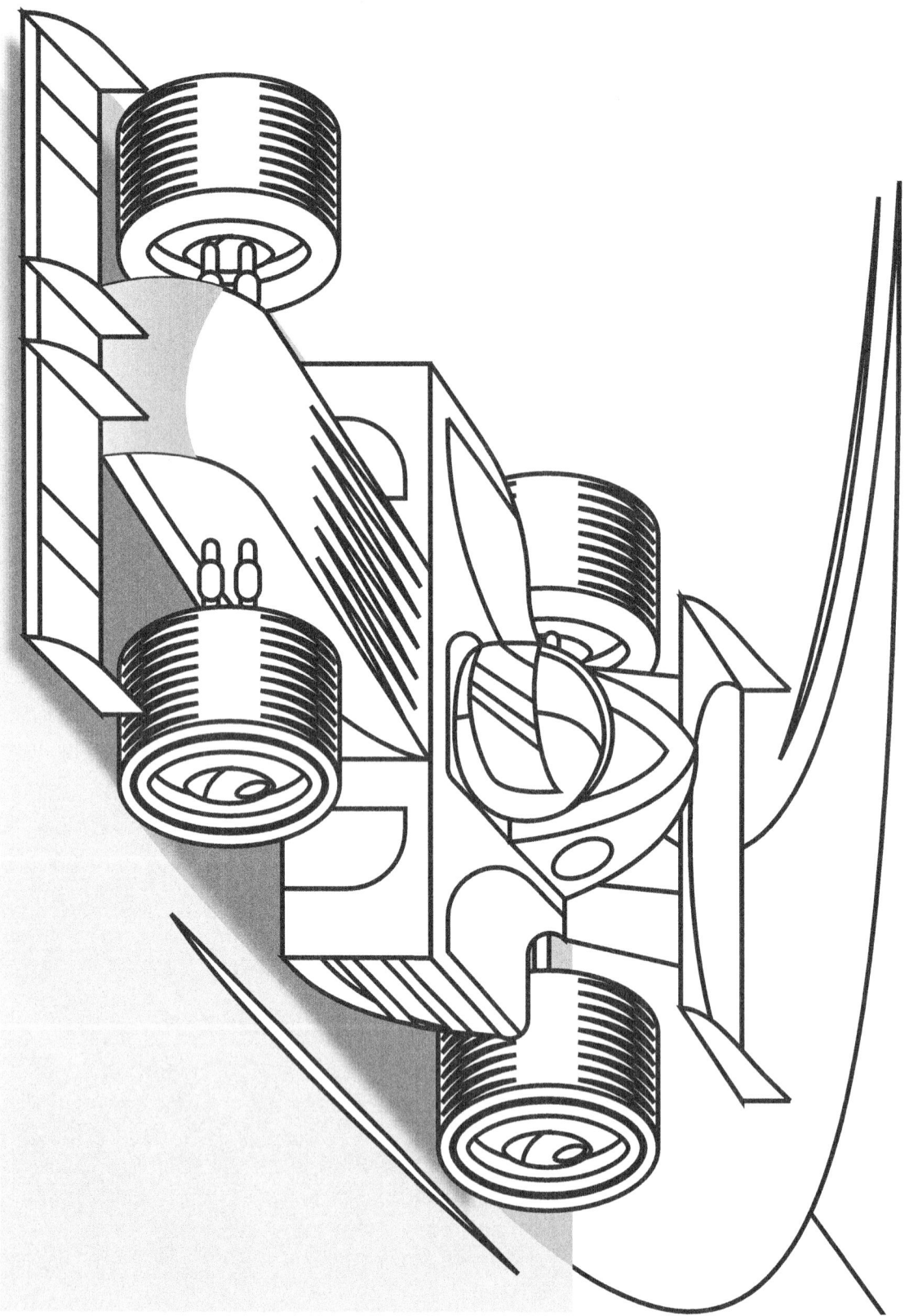

Max Verstappen is the youngest F1 driver, as he attended the first race when he was 17 years

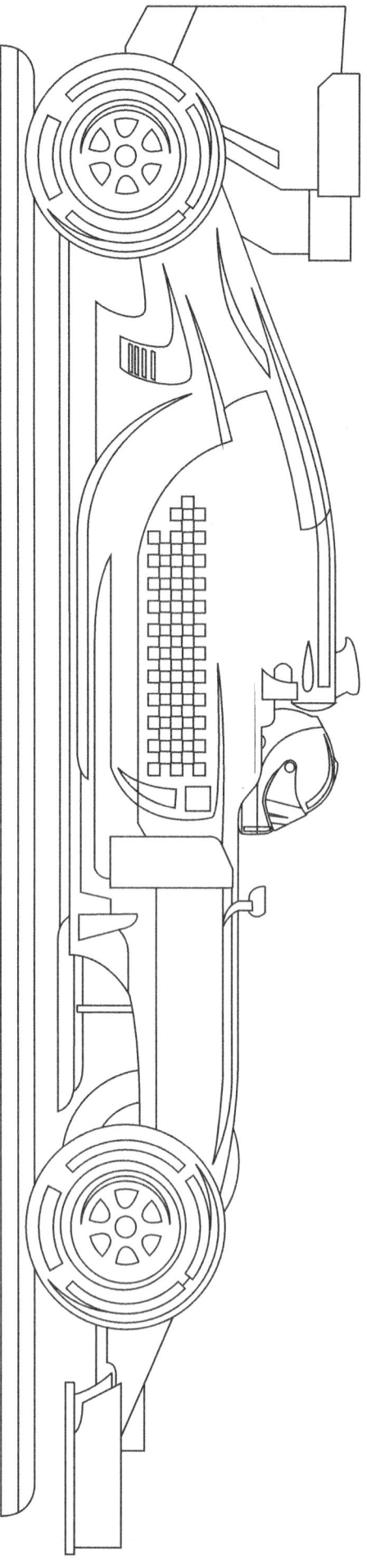

The crew changes tires in 3 seconds

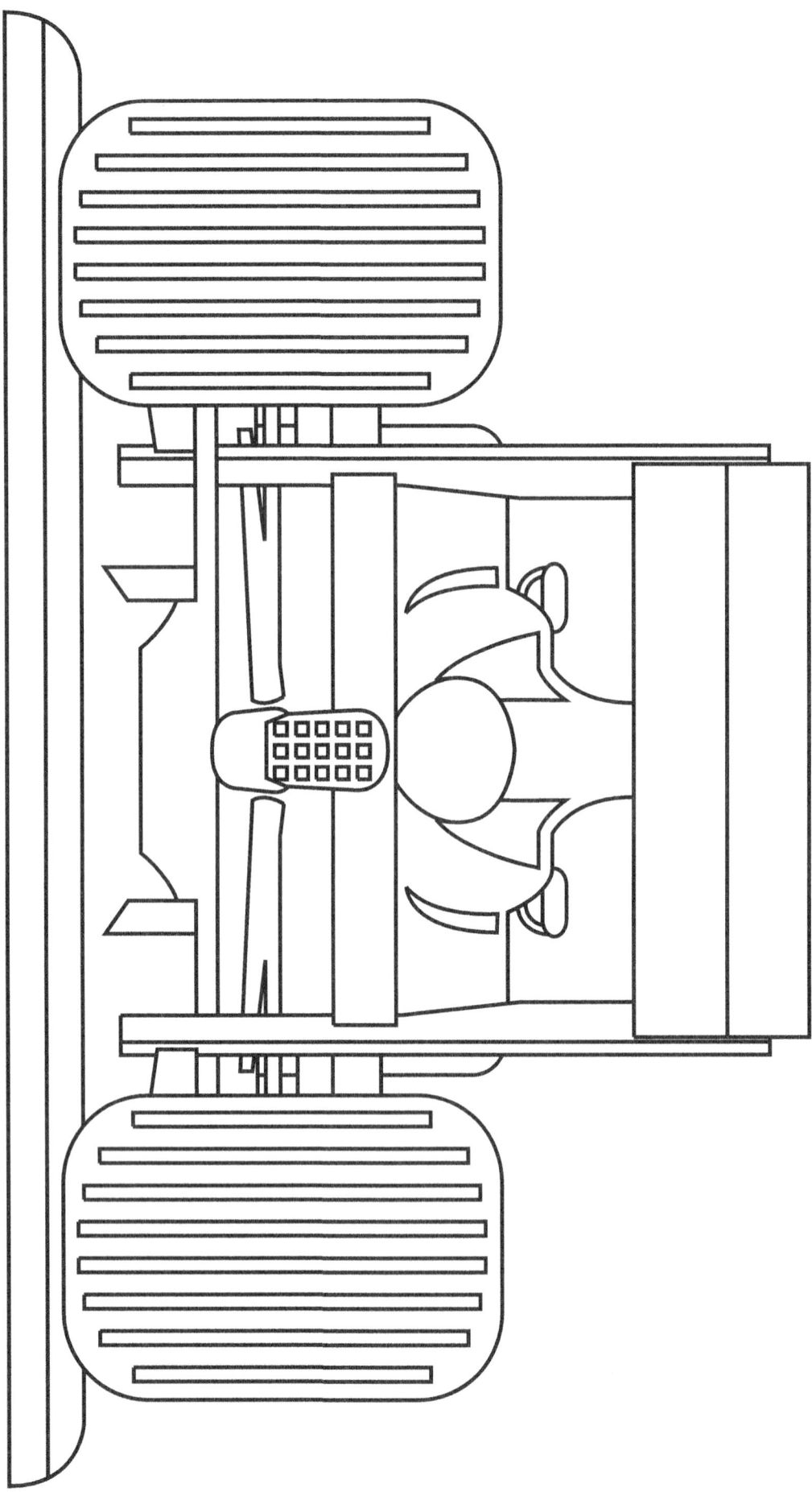

An F1 car can drive upside down

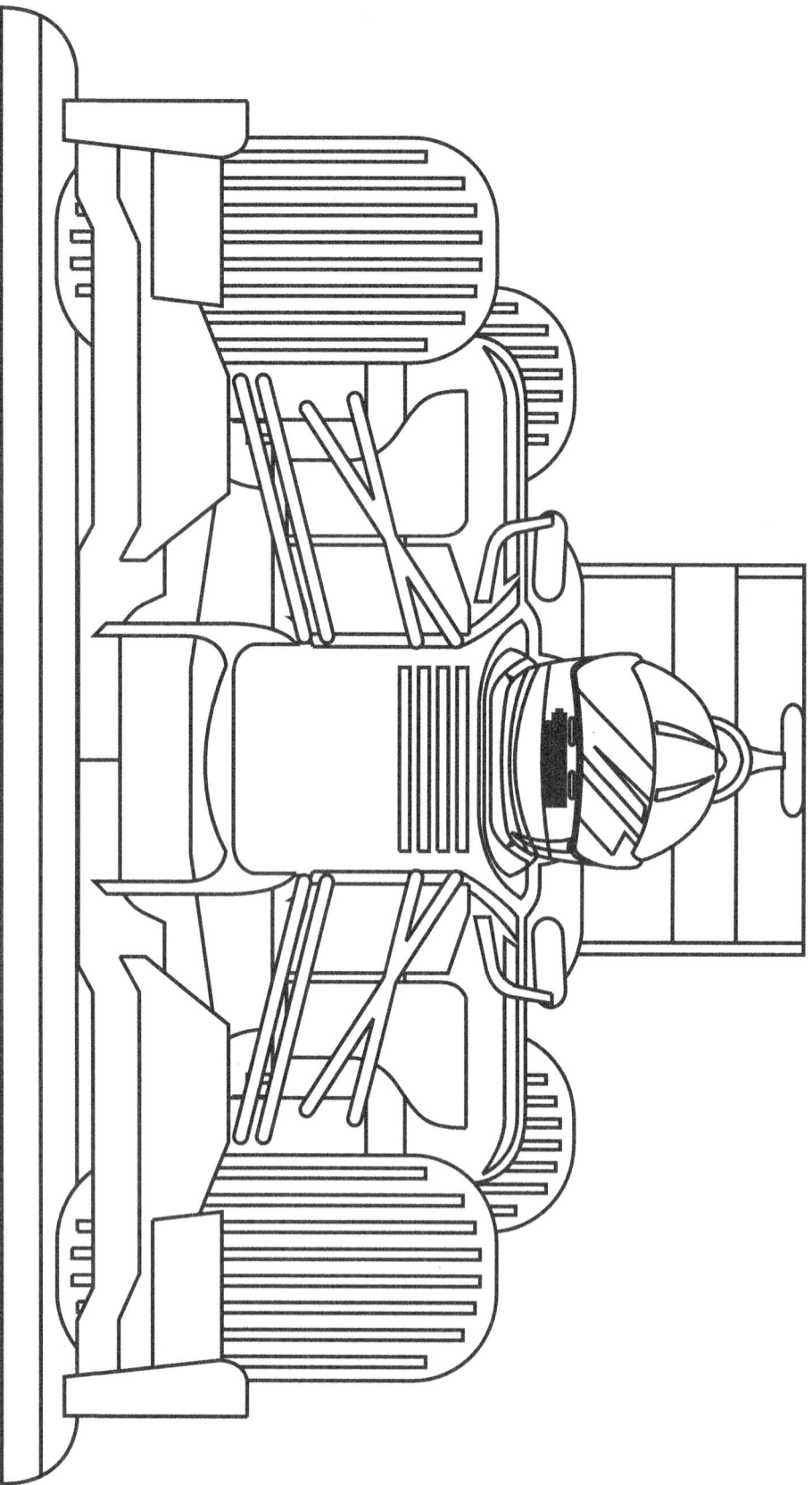

F1 engine lifespan is
less than 5 races

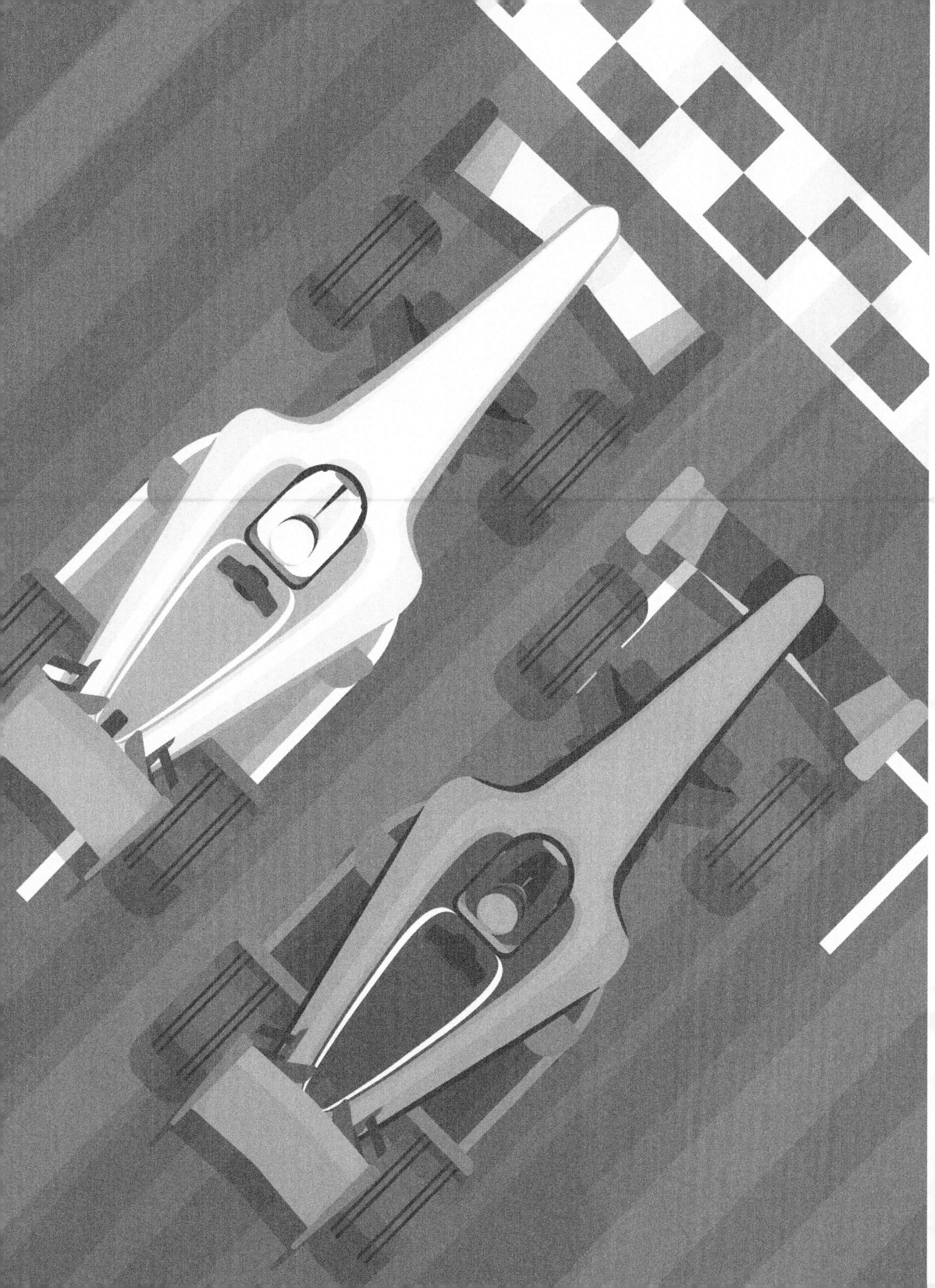

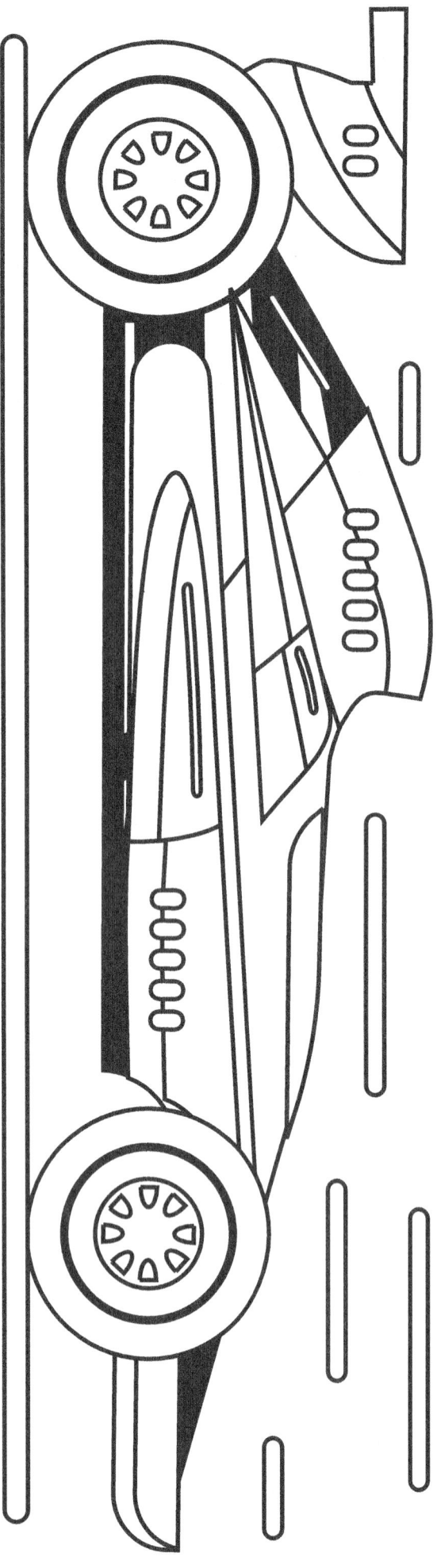

McLaren's Title Drought. Despite spending millions, the last time McLaren won the title was in 2008 when Lewis Hamilton was behind the wheel.

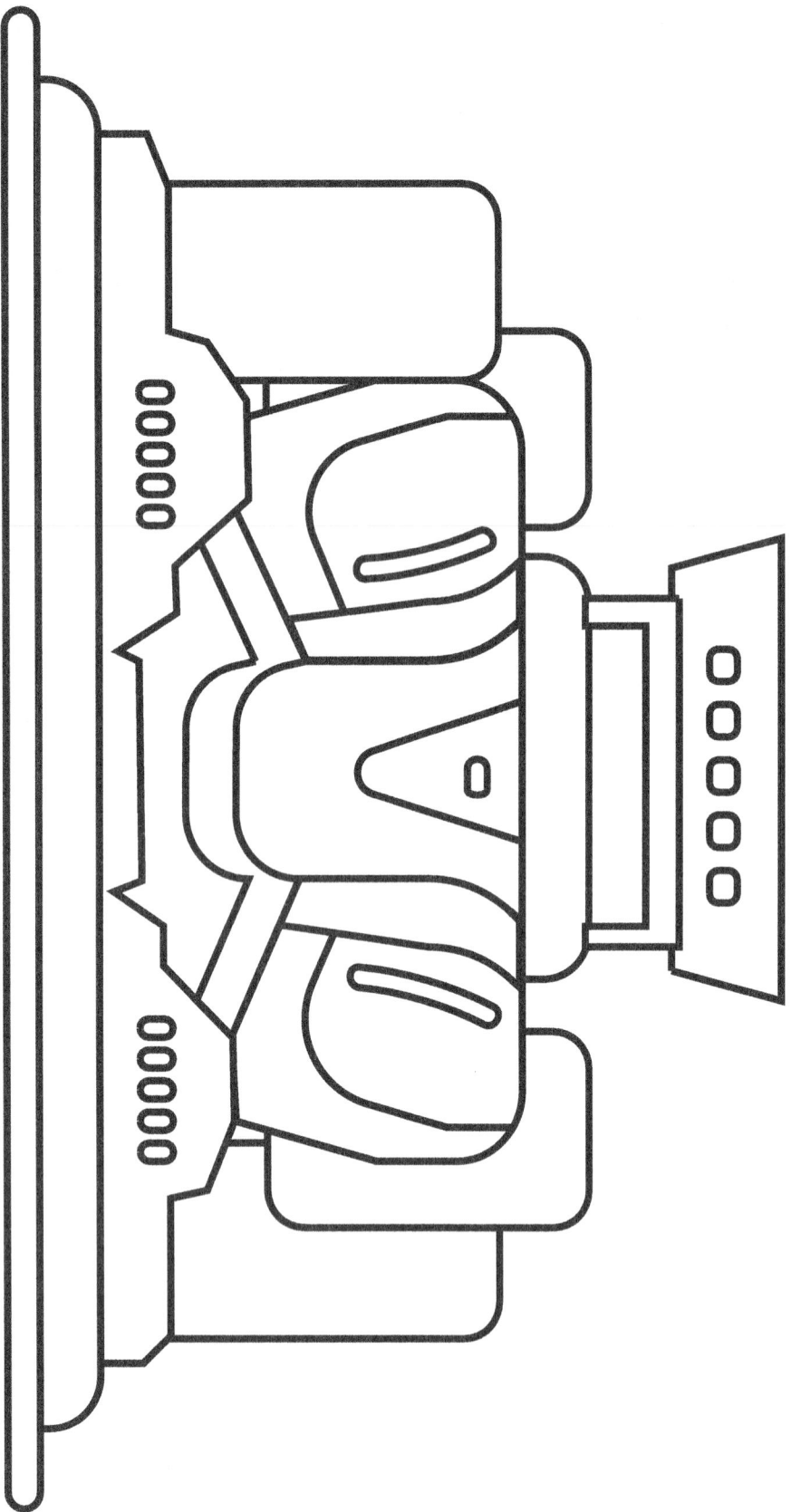

The weight of the car must not be below 728 kg without fuel

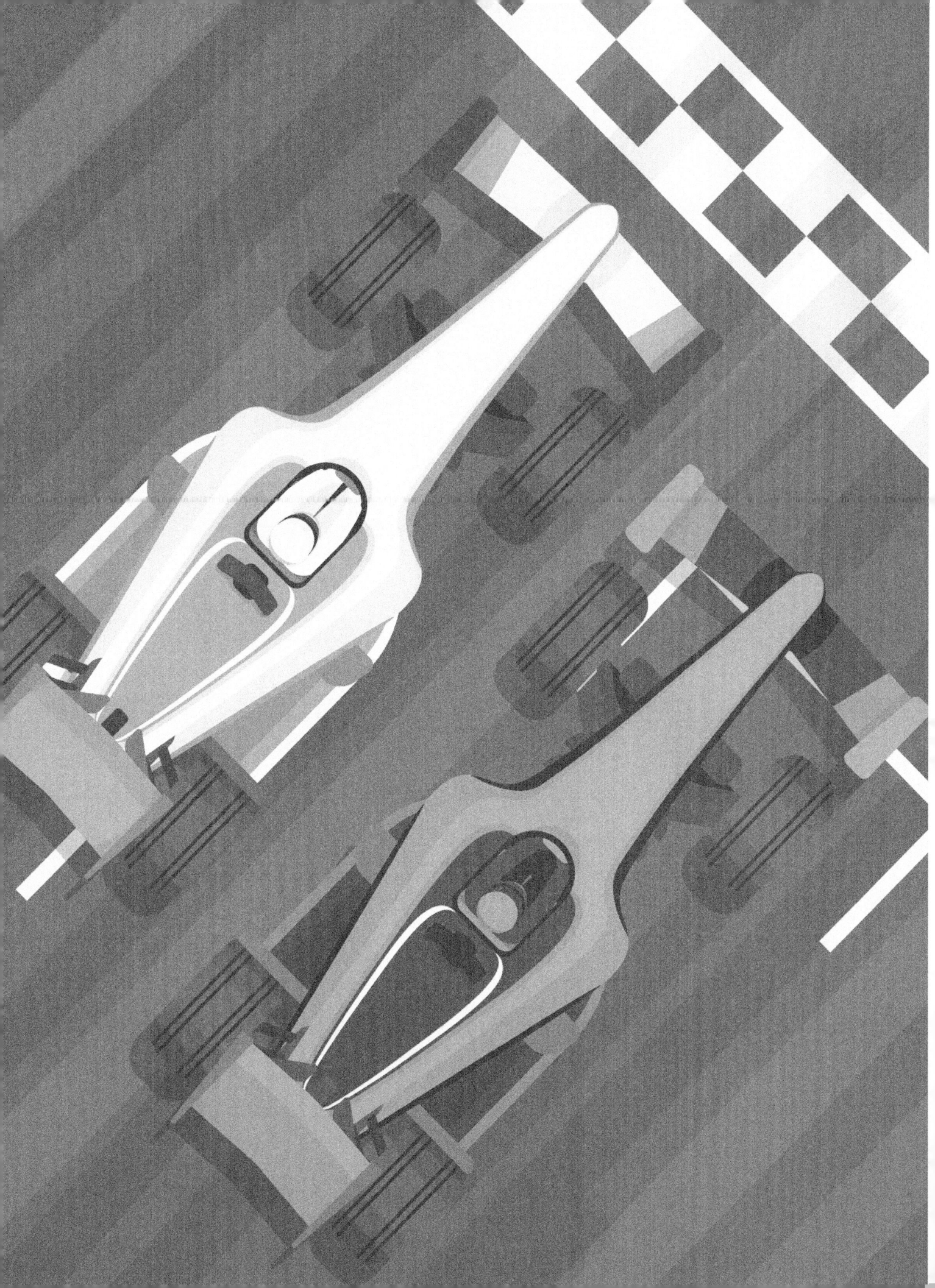

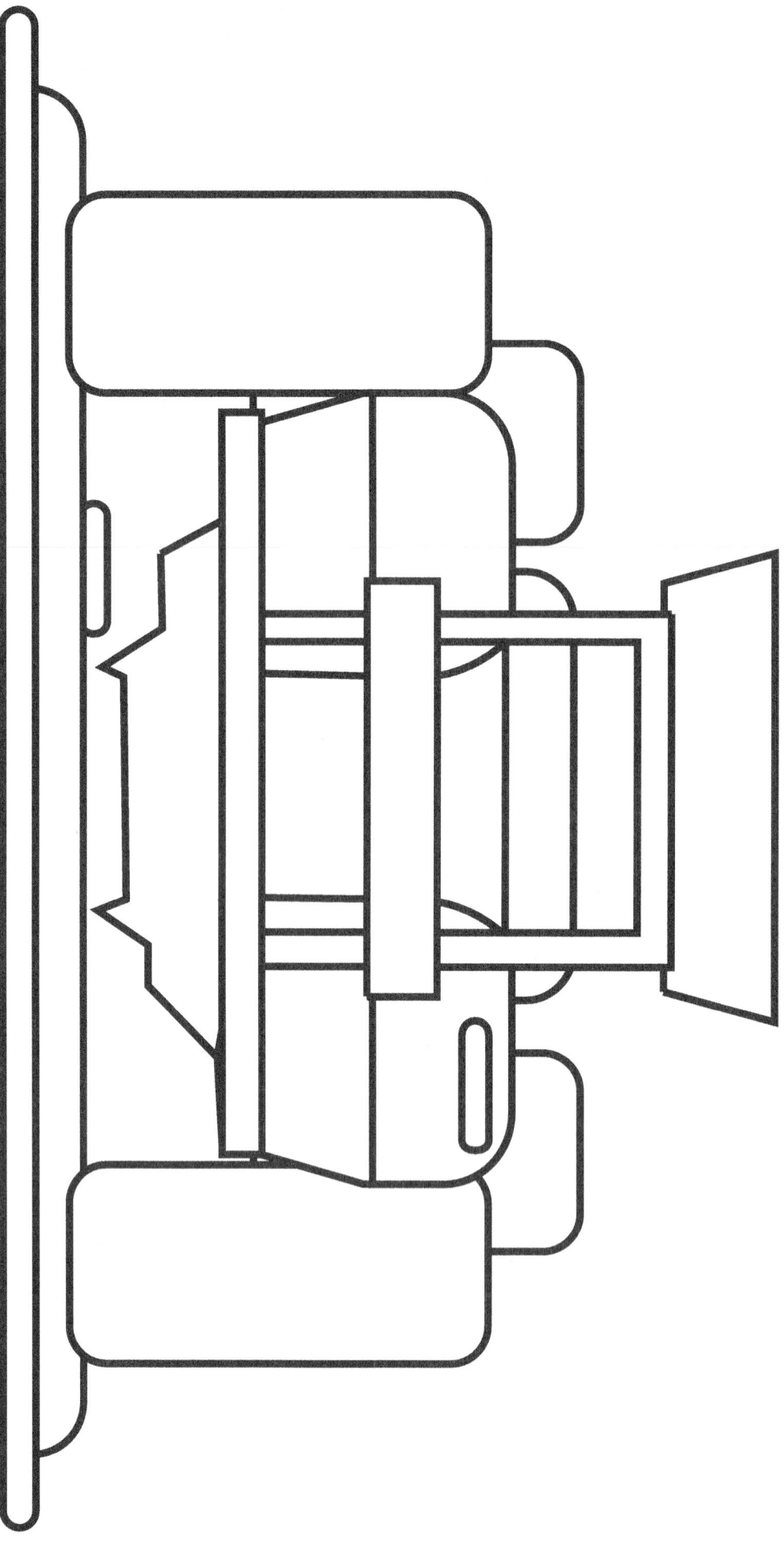

There is only 1 female driver scored a point, her name is Lella Lombardi.

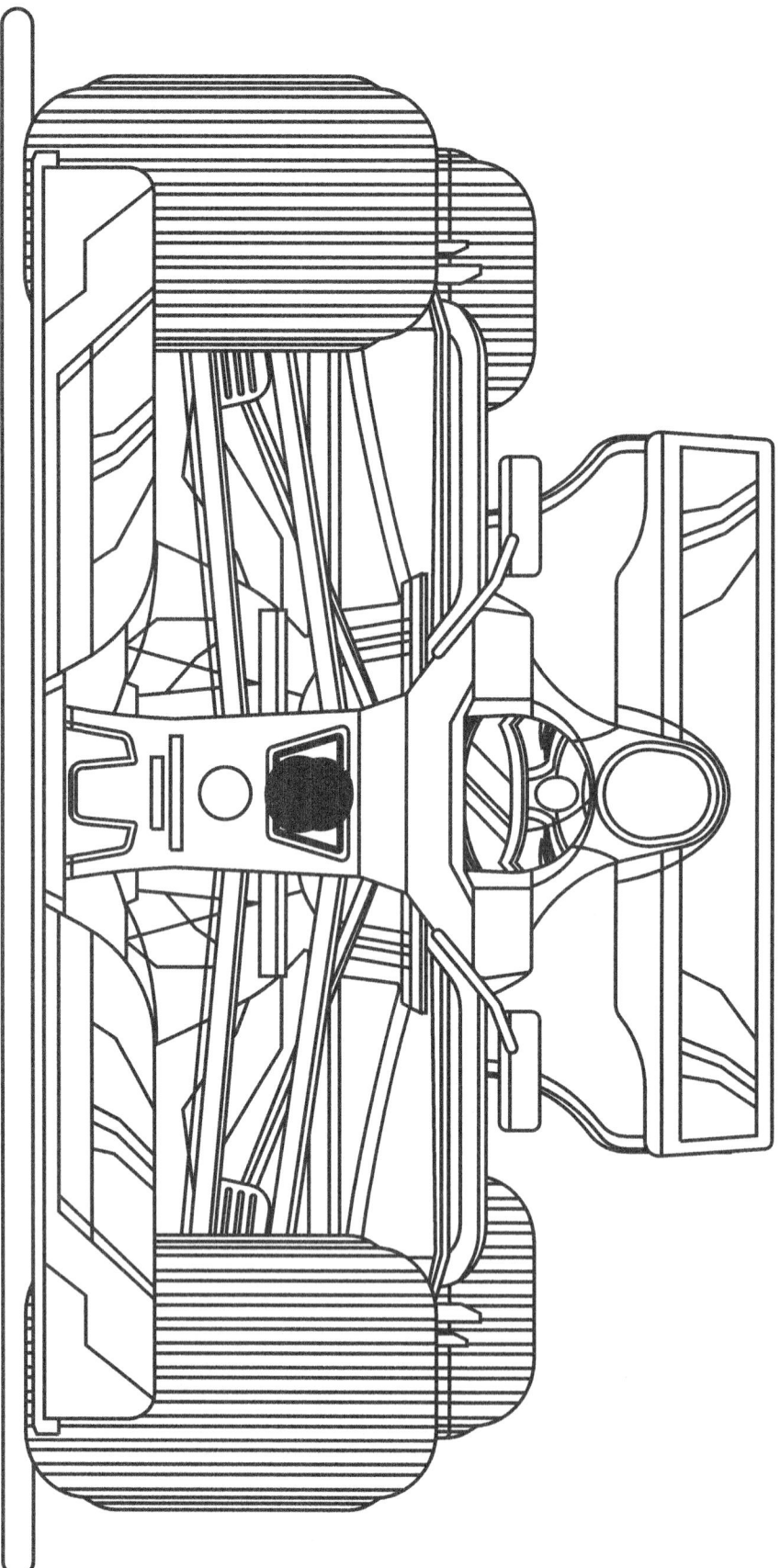

On average a driver loses 4 kg after one race

46 drivers died in an accident

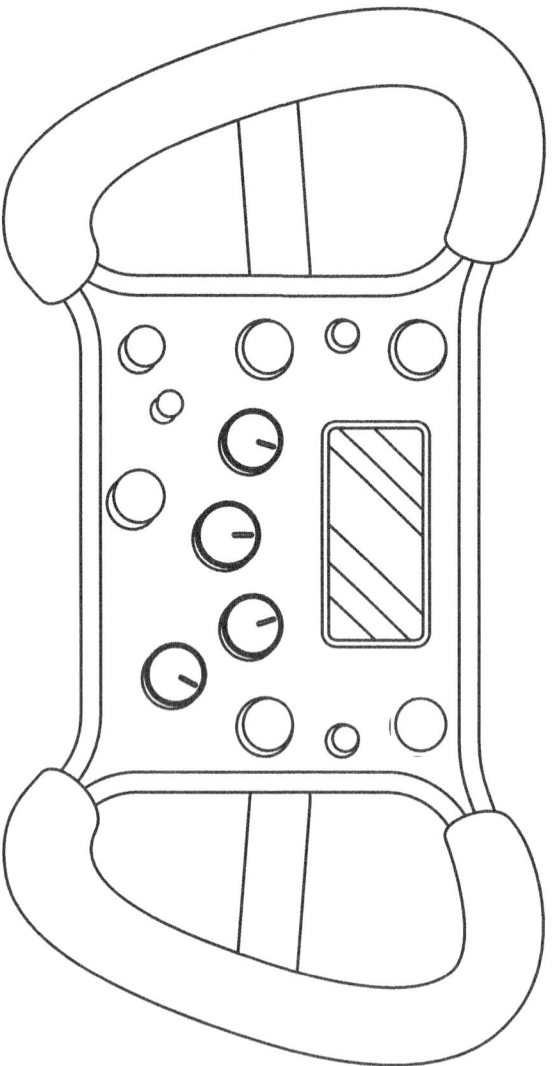

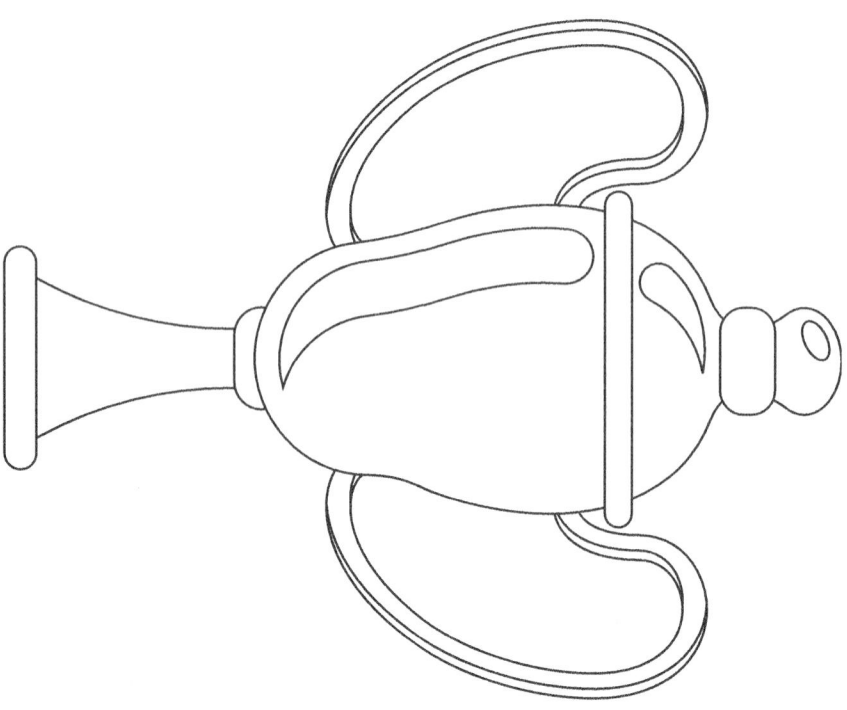

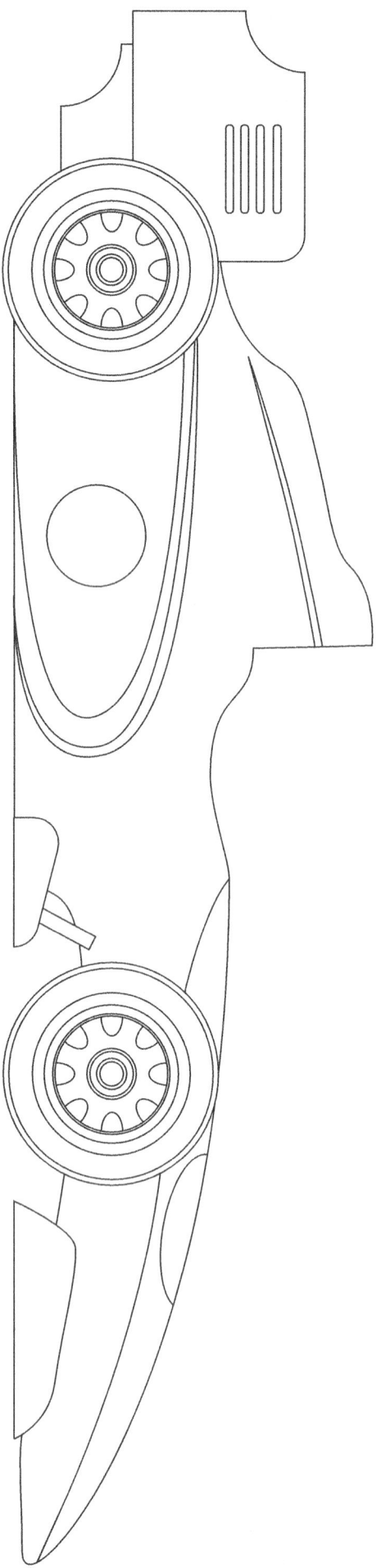

A driver loses 3 liters during a race

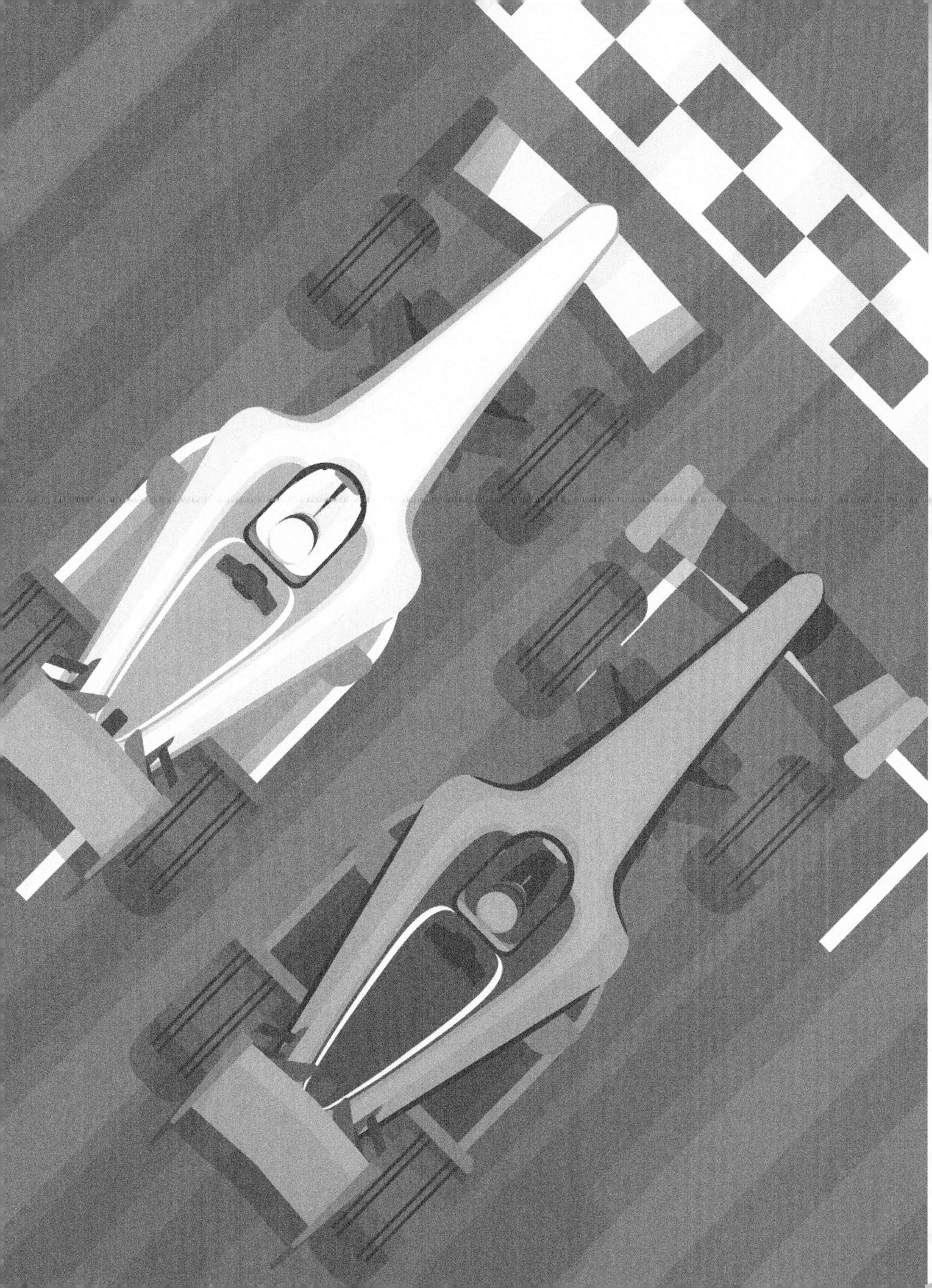

2 **1** **3**

Three people named Hill have
won the World Championship

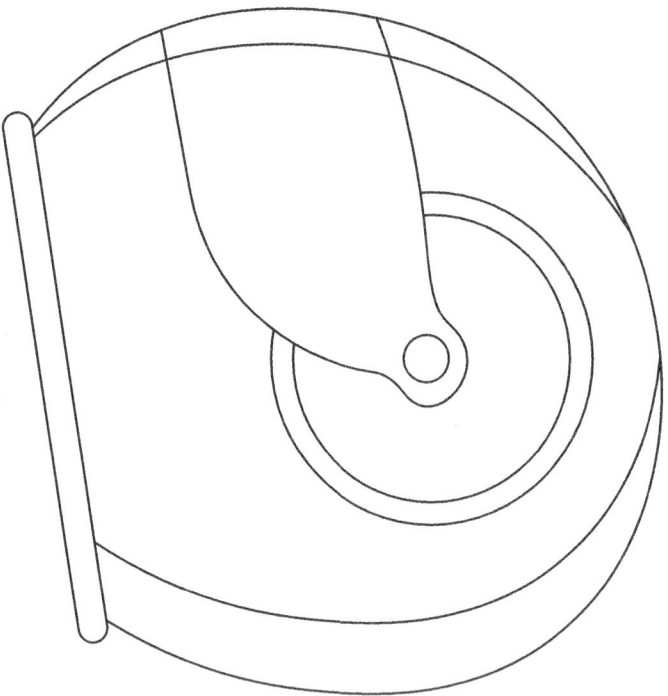

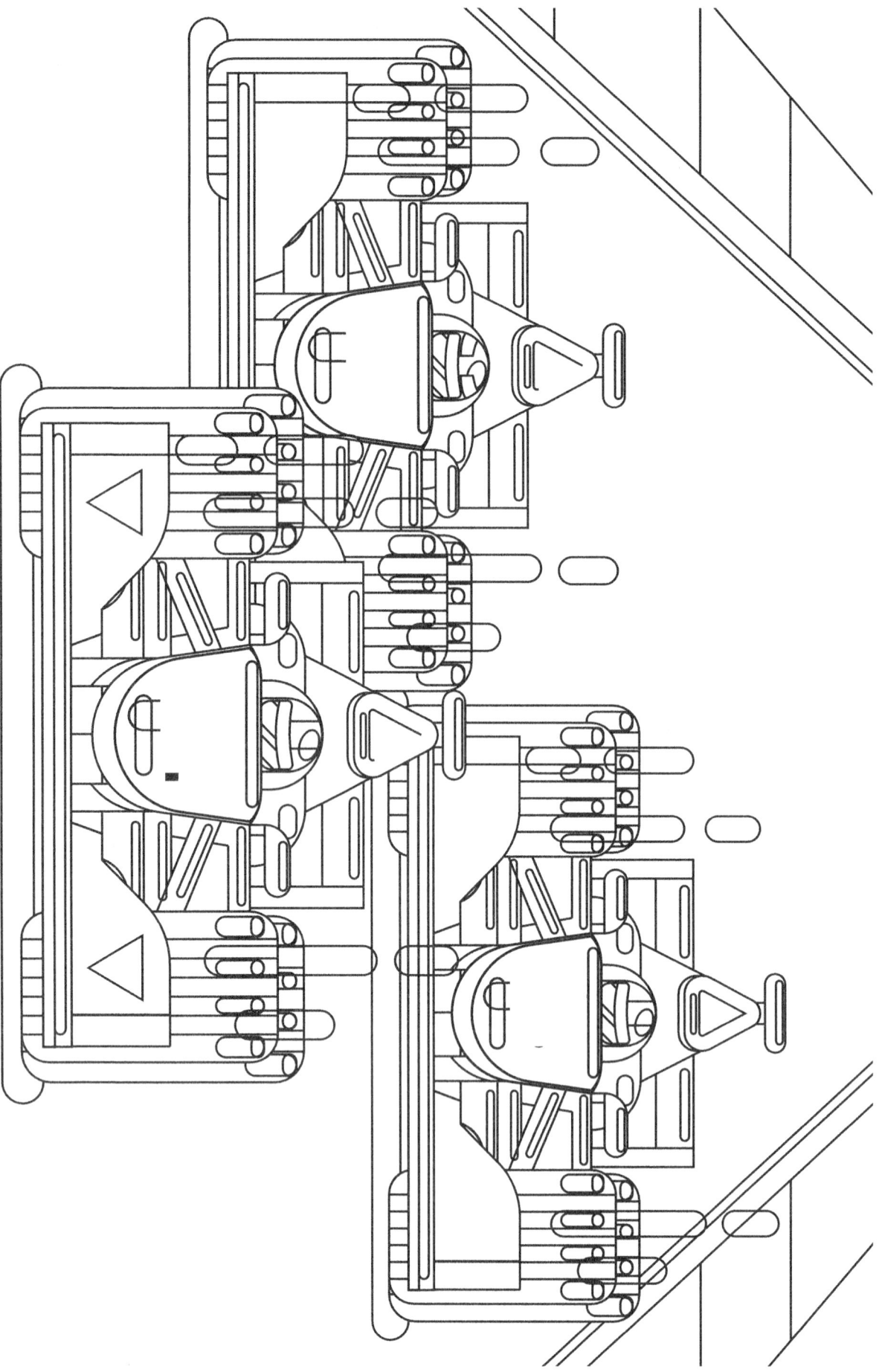

Tires lose 0.5 kg during a race

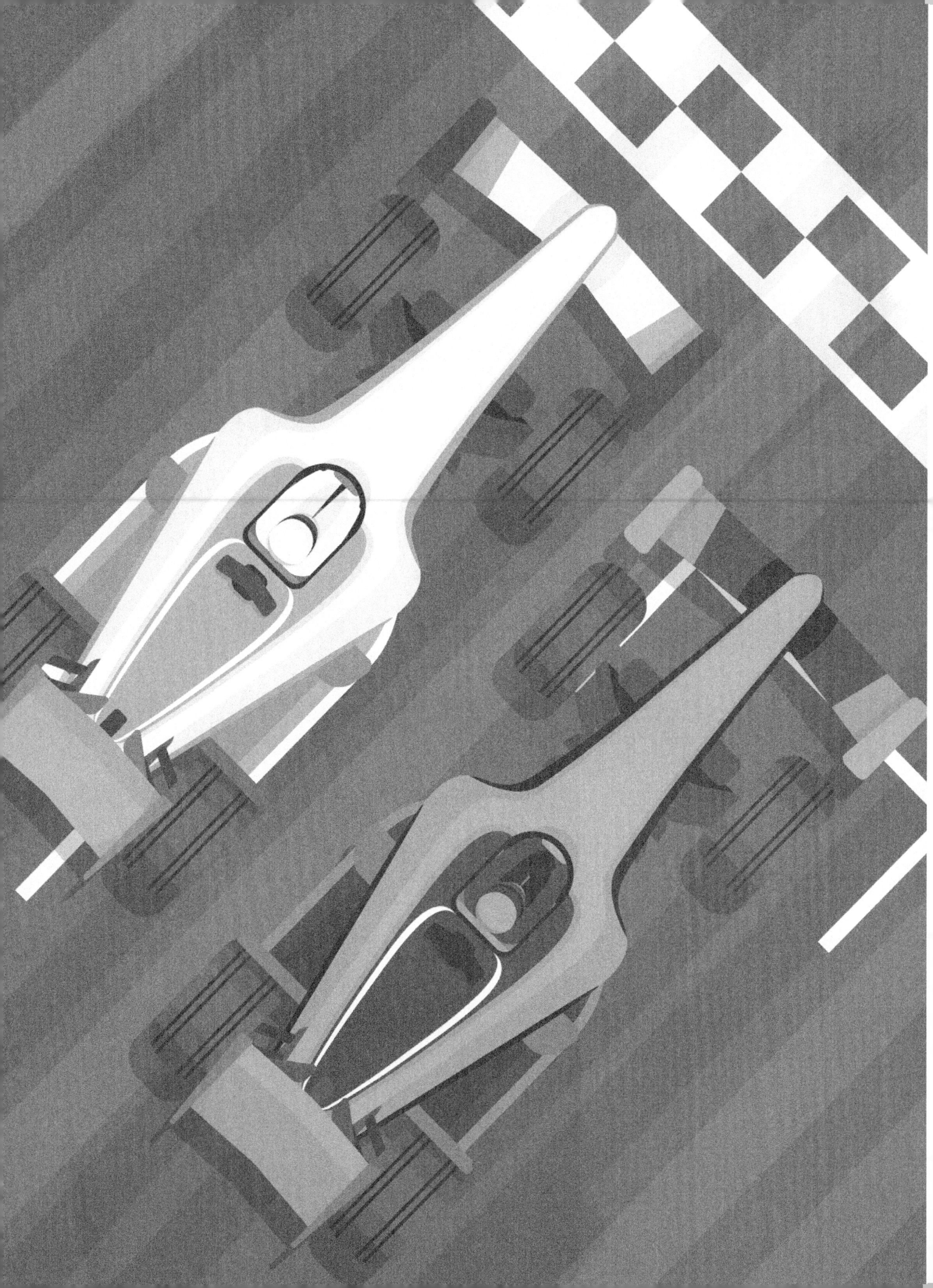

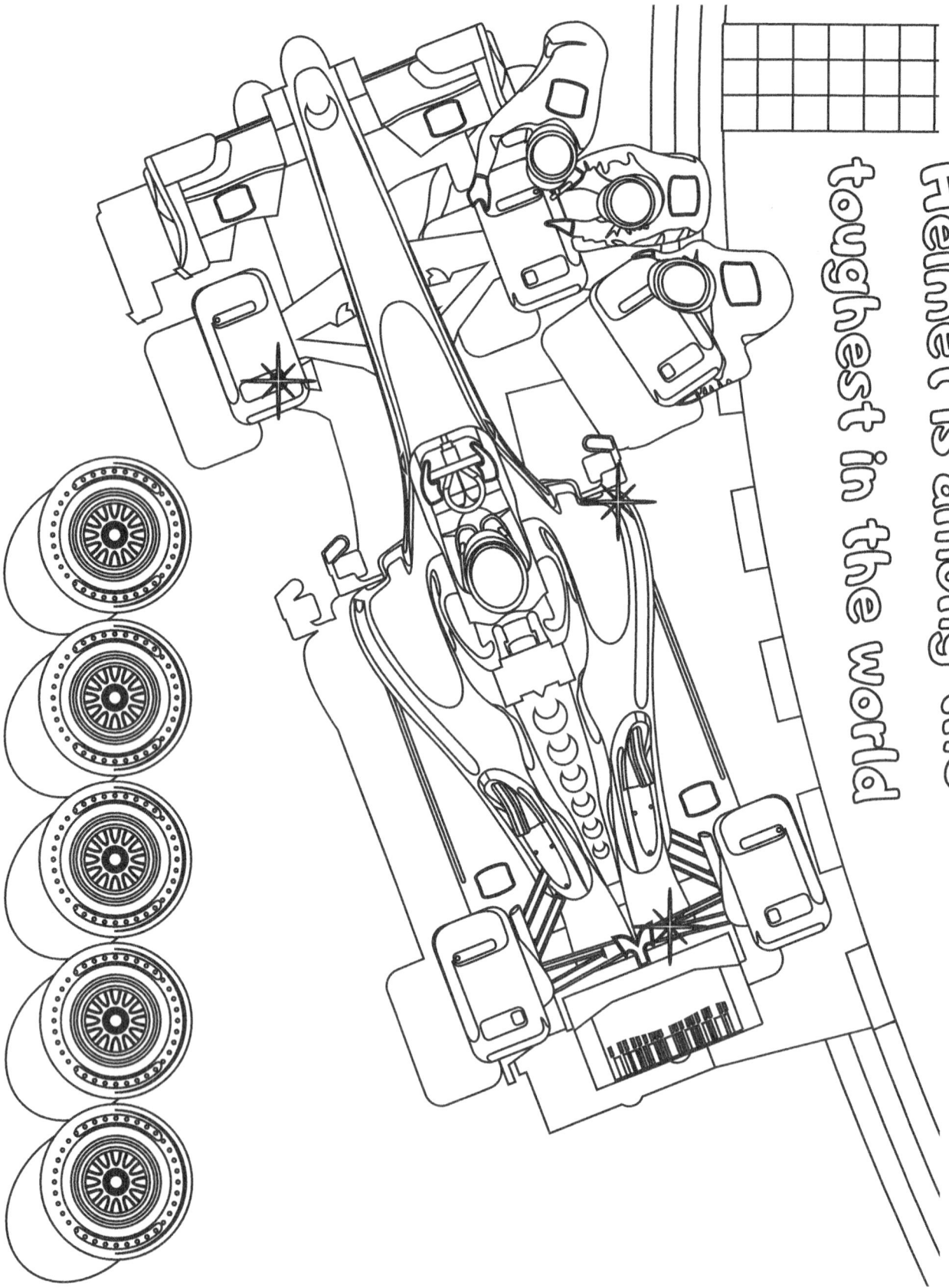

Helmet is among the
toughest in the world

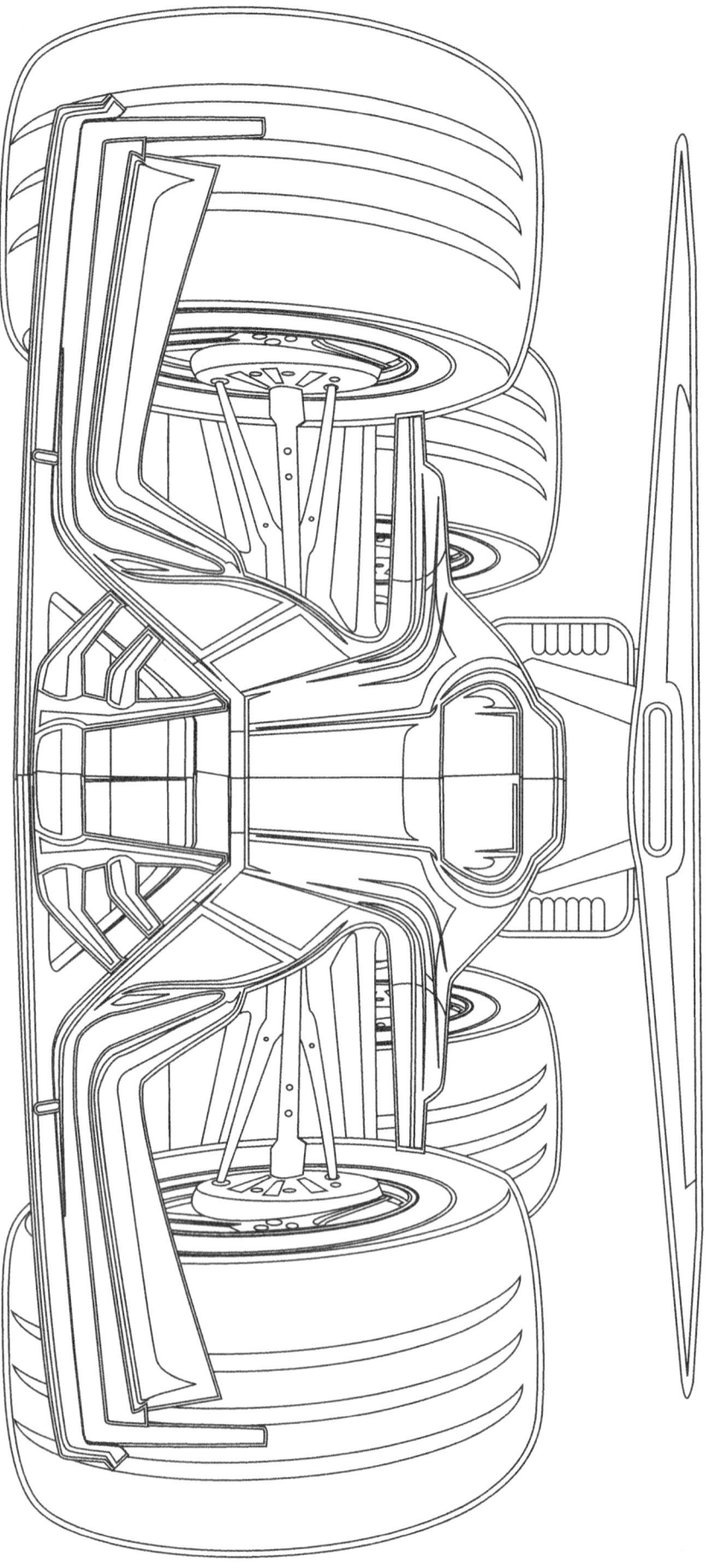

Monza isn't home-race of Ferrari. The circuit in Imola named after Ferrari founder, but now the circuit is no longer held F1 GP

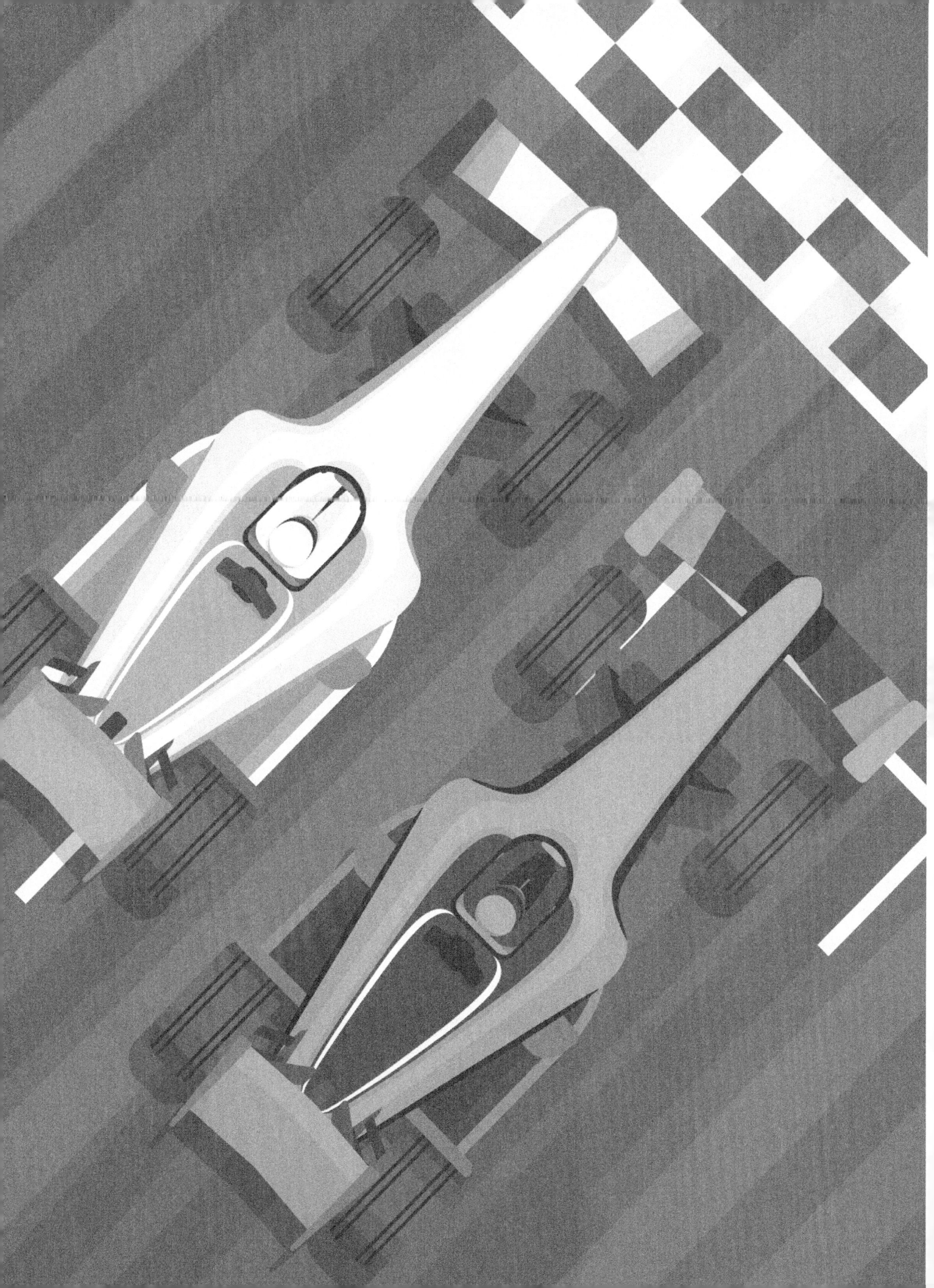

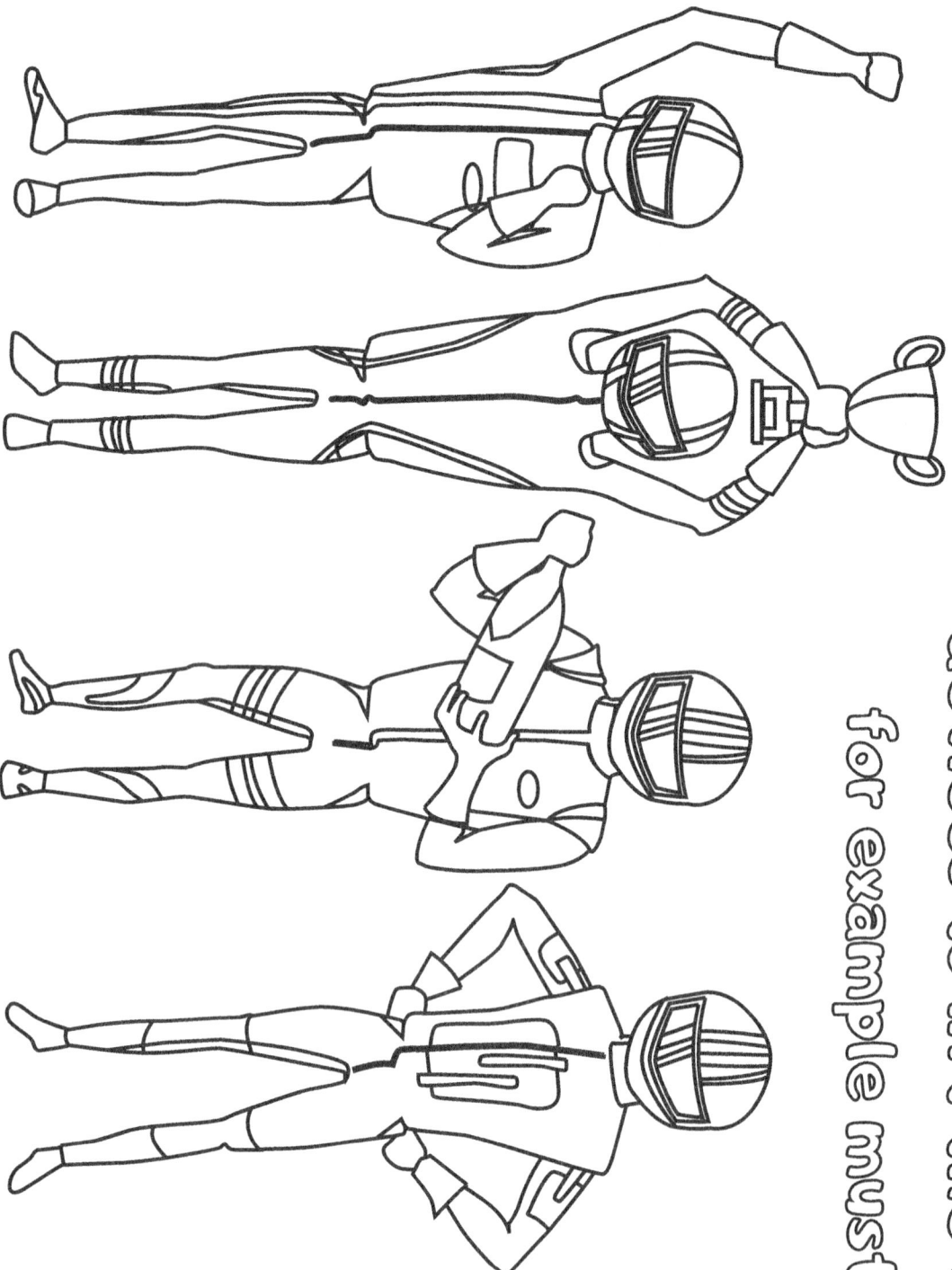

In the pit lane it is not permissible to use powered devices to lift the cars. All jacks for example must be manual.

Small planes are able to take off at slower speeds than F1 cars reach during a race.

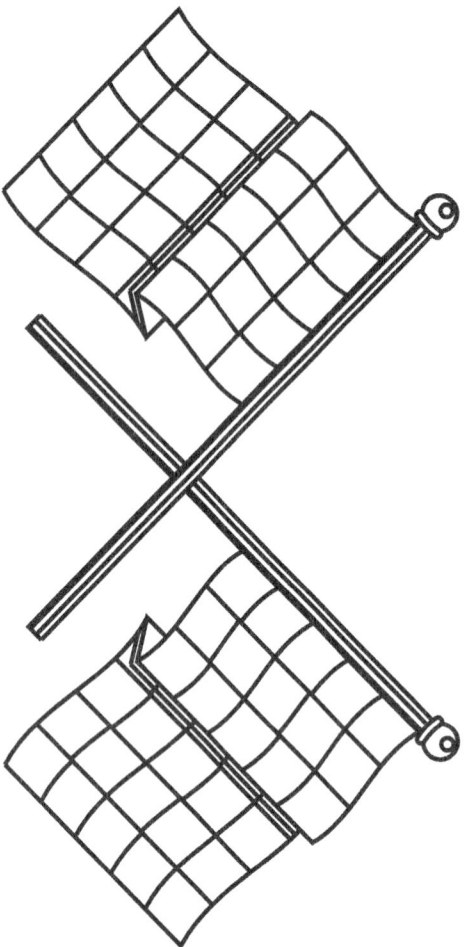

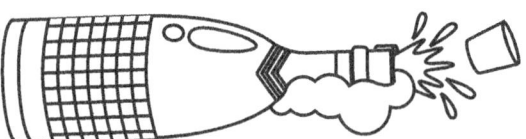

The front suspension of an F1 car can cope with up to 2 tonnes of pressure.

Once a race has finished an F1 car's tyres will still be hot enough to cook an egg on (around 120°C)

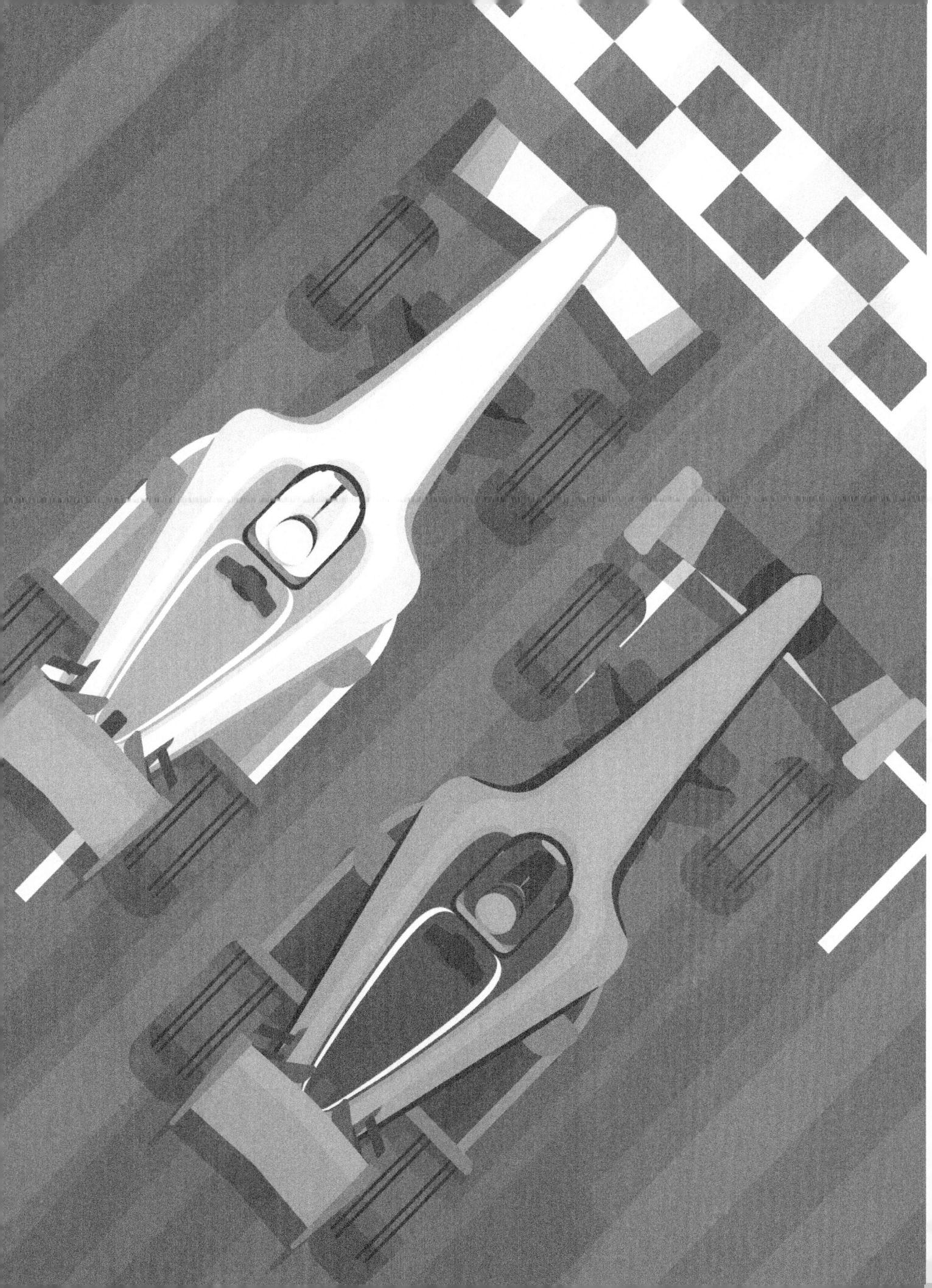

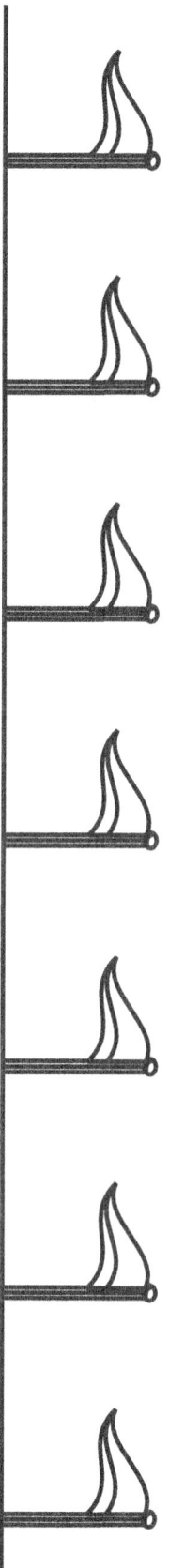

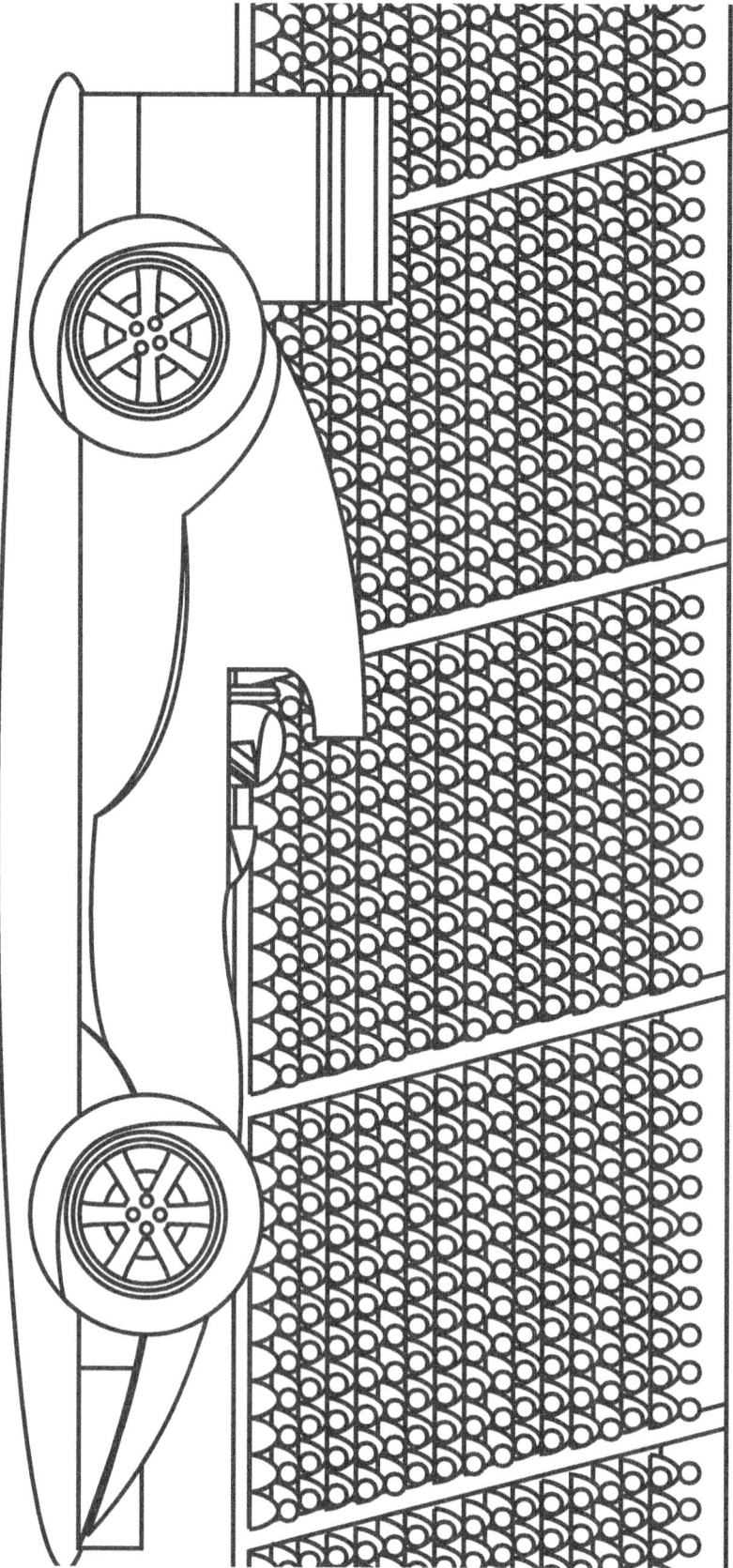

All drivers who wish to compete in F1 must have a FIA Super Licence.

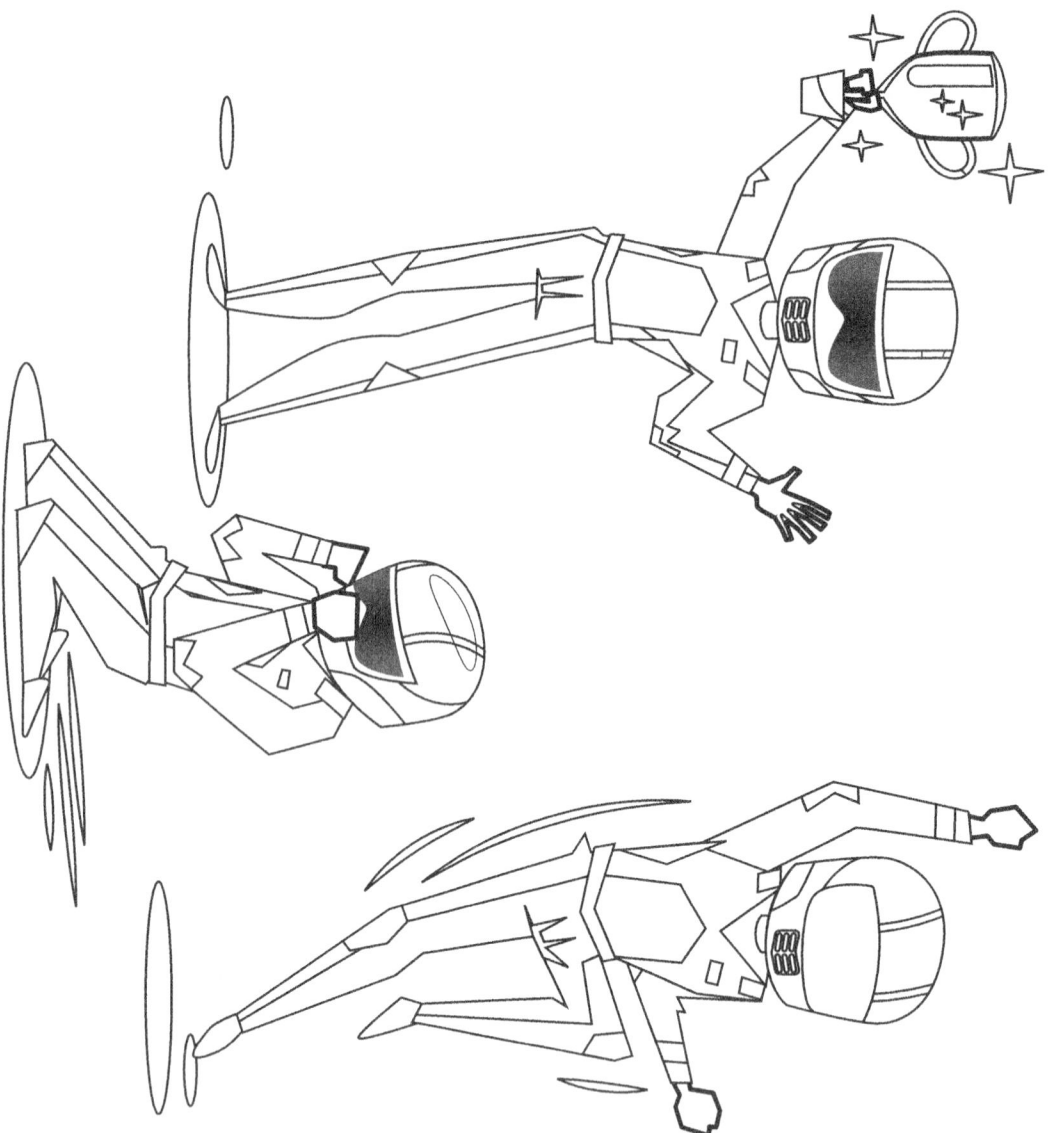

The country with the most F1 Championship winning drivers is the UK with 10 drivers

Since the first Formula One Championship in 1950, 69 countries have hosted a Grand Prix.

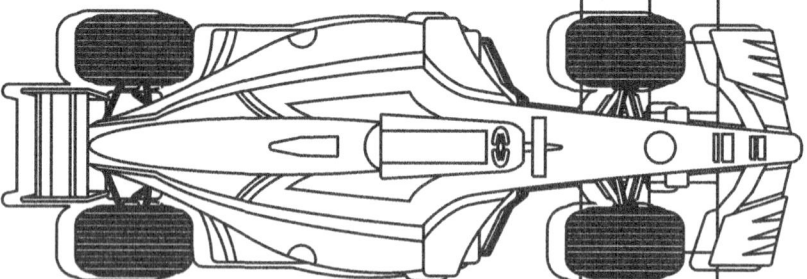

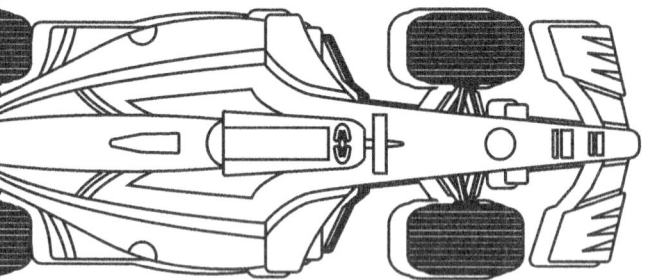

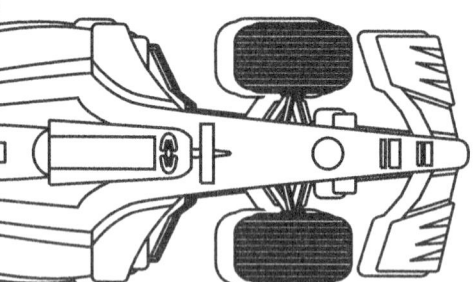

The 1958 Formula 1 Championship experienced the most driver fatalities with four drivers losing their lives in track accidents.

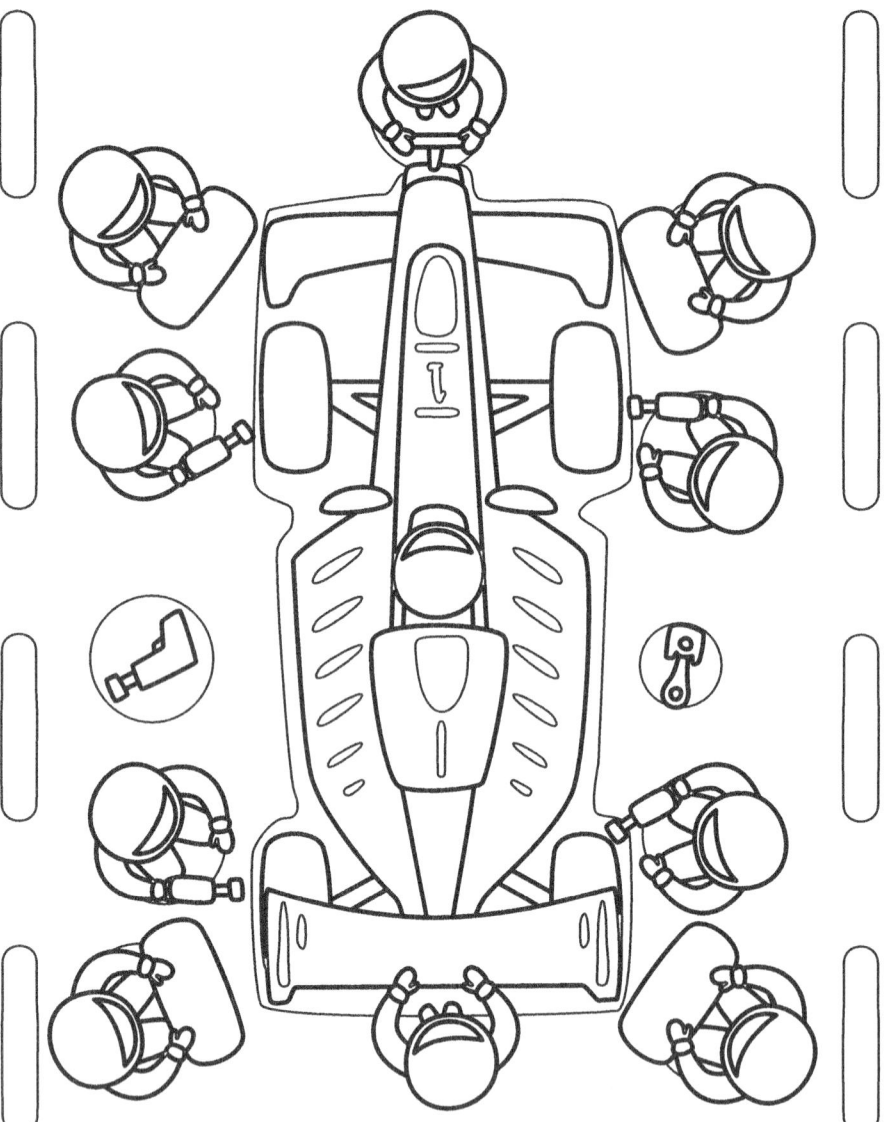

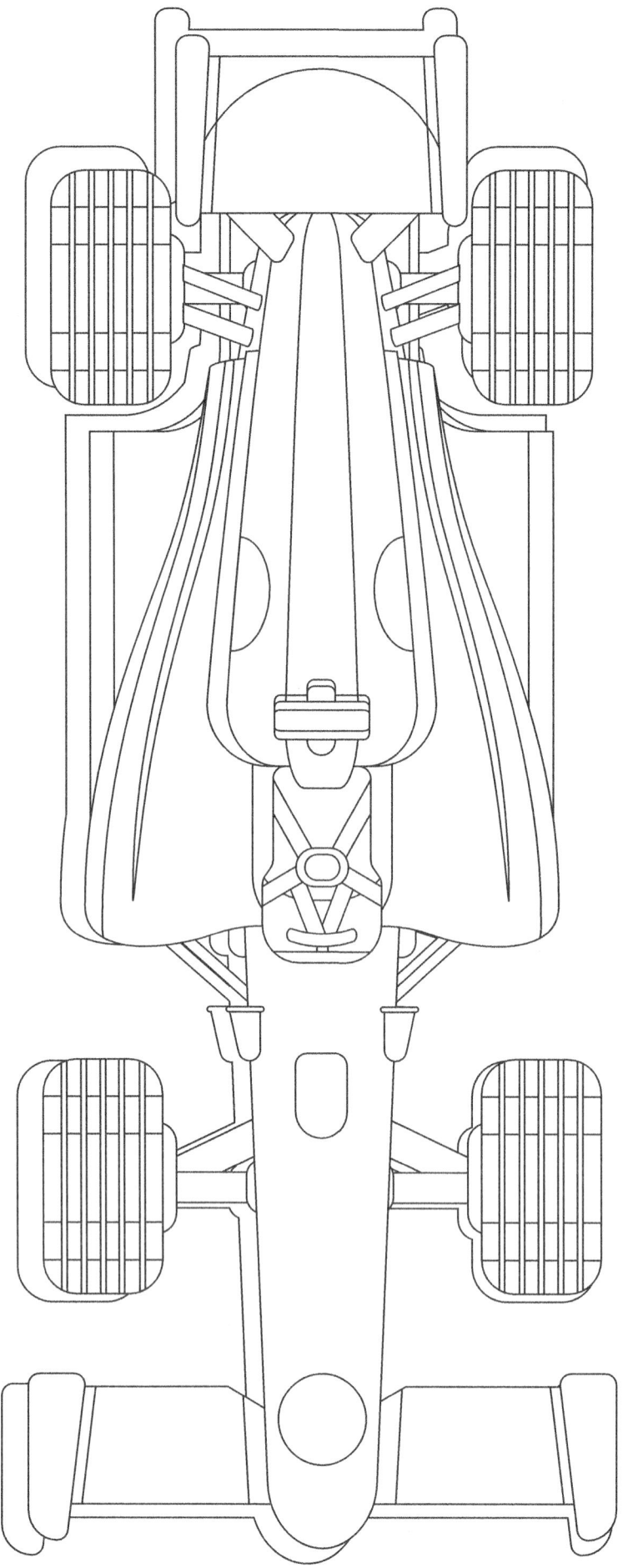

The Yas Marina Circuit in Abu Dhabi has the longest acceleration period of any F1 track in the world at 1,173 metres.

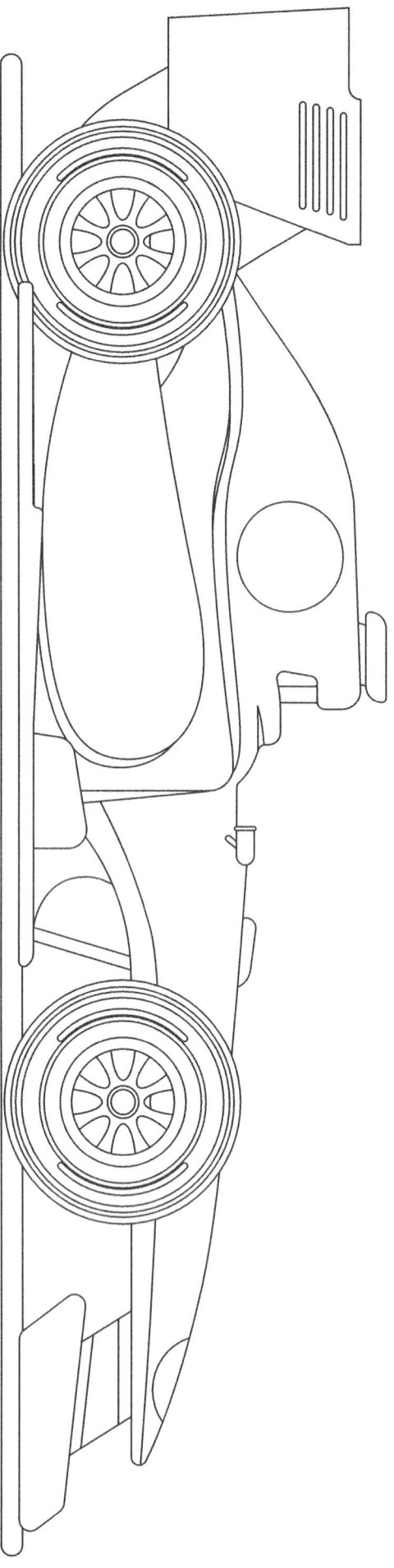

F1 helmets can stand flames of 800°C for at least 45 seconds.

History of Formula 1

Formula one has a very long and rich history, full of drama and danger. We won't be able to fully include here all F1 history, this will be just a brief look into it for people that want to know the basics

Formula 1 starts in the earliest days of motor racing, but in 1946 it became an officially sanctioned category of motorsport. Right from the start, it was meant to be the highest tier of single-seater racing in the world, and it has for the most part lived up to that definition

The word „Formula" is associated with regulations that were set by the sport's governing body, and these rules were changing all the time, sometimes even multiple times during one season. The rules were meant to drive people's innovation as well as increase competition between drivers

Throughout its history, Formula 1 has been powered by just about every engine there is, starting with 1.5-liter supercharged and 4.5-liter naturally-aspirated pre-WWII engines, they were switching between the two kinds of induction systems all the time

There was rumbling V6s and screaming V12s and everything in between. But each year the engineers somehow manage to get even more power

At the beginning Formula 1 was very dangerous. Drivers were living with awareness that they had very high change of not making it to the finish line. In the first decade of this sport, 13 drivers were killed. and 37 more went on to follow until the 1994 Imola Grand Prix, when the death of Ayrton Senna prompted a new wave of safety measures. Today, even in the most violent crashes, great majority of drivers survive but still there are few sad cases when it's just too late. At least F1 is a sport that's constantly innovating thanks to automotive advancement. Since 1950 a lot has changed, production vehicles have benefited from technologies developed and polished in the single-seater cars, such as disc brakes, active suspension, energy recovery systems, improved tires, and better safety equipment. The design of our everyday cars was highly inspired by the work done in the f1 and other motorsports

Some automakers like Ferrari, were also influenced by Formula one, they started selling production vehicles to finance it's efforts in formula 1 and today, Ferrari is definitely one of the most luxury car brand in the history. Formula is also a great source of entertainment, fast cars + competitive and interesting minds has always catched the attention of a viewer. Sometimes even the team bosses and engineers are involved in a celebrity-web filled drama. Memorable crashed and conflicts between particular drivers or teams are still being discussed years and decades after they happened as well as not so mainstream tactics, political debates and ethical discussions about danger associated with this sport.

Formula 1 is still far from perfect, it's plagued with financial issues that can affect small teams or more iconic Grand Prix Venues. Nevertheless, tiny 1.6-liter turbocharged engines produce up to 760 bhp, multiple world champions battle it out wheel-to-wheel every Grand Prix weekend, and the cars go around a track faster than anything else—even the mighty LMP1 cars can't come close to the level of speed, acceleration, braking, and cornering that F1 cars combine in a single package. Our advancing technology is truly extraordinary.

Thanks for reading this, we hope that you're learned something new :D

Best formula one drivers (not in any particular order)

Sebastian Vettel

Total career wins: 53

Total career points: 2985

Formula one Championship wins: 4

Overall podium finish: 120

Nation: Germany

He's currently driving for the redbull racing team of Austria. He debutted in the 2007 United States and achieved 7th position. In the 2009 Formula one season, he raced for Red Bull for the first time and finished as the youngest ever World Driver's Championship runner up

Jenson Button

Total career wins: 1

Total career points: 1235

Formula one Championship wins: 1

Overall podium finish: 1235

Nation: UK

He's currently associated with McLaren and was the 2009 Formula One World Champion for the brown GP F1 team.

In his career with McLaren, BAR, Honda and Mercedes till now, he has won 15 Grand Prix along with 1140 career points and 8 pole positions_

Michael Schumacher

Total career wins: 91

Total career points: 1566

Formula one Championship wins: 7

Overall podium finish: 155

Nation: Germany

World's first billionare athlete is now a retired German fl driver. He has won his last race in the 2006 Chinese Grand Prix. For sure, he's one of the greatest Formula 1 drivers of all time. Schumacher suffered from a serious cerebral injury in 2013 while skiing and was in coma from december 2013 until june 2014

Ayrton Senna

Total career wins: 41

Total career points: 620

Formula one Championship wins: 3

Overall podium finish: 80

Nation: Brazil

Fastest driver of the 90's. Senna made his debut in 1984 at the brazillian Grand Prix where he qualified as the 17th. He first won the title of Formula One World Championship for Drivers in the 39th season of FIA F1 motor racing in 1988. He died due to significant blood loss after a tragic accident on the track in San Marino Grand Prix

Stirling Moss

Total career wins: 16

Total career points: 185

Formula one Championship wins: 0

Overall podium finish: 24

Nation: UK

During his career from 1951 to 1961, he teamed with Mercedes-Benz, Vanwall, and Maserati and also participated in 67 international races. He was the first British driver to win an F1 British Grand Prix, while riding a british made car. Unfortunately, he had no world championship record and his career stopped after being partially paralized in 1962

Lewis Hamilton

Total career wins: 84

Total career points: 3431

Formula one Championship wins: 6

Overall podium finish: 151

Nation: UK

This driver currently races for the Mercedes-AMG Petronas Motorsport at Formula One. Has now has 84 race victories along 151 podium finishes under his name. He also bagged the DHL Fastest Lap Award four times till now. Hamilton received both Autosport International Racing Driver Award and the Autosport British Competition of the year award seven times each

Alain Prost

Total career wins: 51

Total career points: 768

Formula one Championship wins: 4

Overall podium finish: 106

Nation: France

He started his leagcy in the 1980 Argentine Grand Prix. In his 2nd race in the 1981 French Grand Prix, he won his first Grand Prix title. Prost won the Formula One Driver's Championship four times in 1985, 1986, 1989, 1993. The 1993 German Grand Prix was the last title he won

Fernando Alonso

Total career wins: 32

Total career points: 1899

Formula one Championship wins: 2

Overall podium finish: 97

Nation: Spain

Alonso is know as the third-youngest driver ever to debut in the international event in F1 history. In the 2001 Australian Grand Prix he drove for the first time. Alonso participated in his last racing championship in the 2014 Belgian Grand Prix where he finished as 4th. According to the new rule of F1 GP for the 2014 session, Alonso picked number 14 considering it to be lucky for him

Thank you for choosing our book!

We've worked really hard to deliver the best quality product to you

If you liked it, consider leaving an honest review on Amazon (scroll down to the bottom of our product page and click on: „Write a customer review"

To claim your 30 free printable coloring pages with cars visit:

coloringpages.wixsite.com/cars